Road to the Rainbow

A Personal Journey to Recovery from an Eating Disorder Survivor

by
Meredith Seafield Grant

CCB Publishing
British Columbia, Canada

Today...I smile at Life

Today...I feel Life

Today...I embrace Life

The darkness is over...I have found Life's Rainbow

Road to the Rainbow: A Personal Journey to Recovery from an
Eating Disorder Survivor

Copyright ©2008 by Meredith Seafield Grant
ISBN-13 978-0-9809191-7-2
Second Edition

Library and Archives Canada Cataloguing in Publication

Grant, Meredith Seafield, 1965-
Road to the Rainbow: A personal journey to recovery from an eating
disorder survivor / written by Meredith Seafield Grant. – 2nd ed.
ISBN 978-0-9809191-7-2
Also available in electronic format.
1. Grant, Meredith Seafield, 1965- --Health. 2. Eating disorders--Patients--
Biography. I. Title.
RC552.E18G73 2008   616.85'260092   C2008-903272-1

Cover design by Susan Butler: www.brandcentraldesign.com

Publisher: CCB Publishing
             British Columbia, Canada
             www.ccbpublishing.com

DEDICATION

In memory of Dr. Doug Shrives.

I also dedicate this book to you the reader
because you are ready to begin.
Helping at least one person realize life is worth living
will have served its purpose.
I hope it is you.

FOREWORD

Eating disorders are misunderstood, massively destructive illnesses robbing mostly young women of their health, spirit and future. It is estimated that over six million women and half a million men have a clinical eating disorder at some point in their lives. While there is a wealth of literature on the biopsychosocial understanding of the disorders, little has been written on the process of recovery. We have much to learn from these accounts, and Meredith Seafield Grant has written a triumphant one.

Meredith has beaten many of the odds that were against her. Her early experience of sexual abuse, repeated hospitalizations and "treatment failures", the chronic course of her illness, the multiple symptoms of anorexia, bulimia and over eating all would have discouraged professional and personal supporters. Yet Meredith has succeeded in reclaiming her health, and lives a full and productive life.

Road to the Rainbow: A Personal Journey to Recovery from an Eating Disorder Survivor is a testimonial with many of the good qualities of a testimonial, and none of the bad. Meredith's story does not glamorize eating disorders, nor does it sensationalize the extremes in behaviour that often incite others to compare and compete. Instead, Meredith focuses on the day to day moments and strategies that have lifted her forward step by step, so that today she can say with confidence that she is recovered.

Meredith starts with hope, and humility and gratitude. Her story is not a "fix" for everyone, but her experience will have something for everyone searching for a way out of an eating disorder. She states that recovery is a process, a process of self-expression that is facilitated by all manner of experiences. For Meredith it involved a hunger strike, self-disclosure, admitting there is a problem, and above all honesty: honesty with a close therapist, her family and friends, and herself. Meredith's story is filled with intentional steps toward rebuilding a sense of self. The emerging person that Meredith becomes defends a positive attitude and making careful choices, all leading toward health.

Exceptional is her account of the use of affirmations, alternative mind/body therapies, journaling, and taking care of her environment.

This book is filled with a fierce sense of determination, optimism and tenacity. As Meredith quotes, "There never was a rainbow without a fall of rain." It is her time for the rainbow; there has been enough rain.

Ann Kerr, B.Sc.O.T. (C)
Program Director, Sheena's Place, 1996-2006
Assistant Professor, Department of Psychiatry
Lecturer, Department of Occupational Therapy
University of Toronto
Toronto, Ontario, Canada

TO THE READER
SURVIVING AN EATING DISORDER

This book is about a journey to recovery, hence the title *Road to the Rainbow.*

It begins with my past, and describes events in my life and how they led to the development of eating disorders.

Road to the Rainbow is not about recovery from any specific disorder. I have been, through the years, an overeater, an anorexic and a bulimic, switching from one to the other. What I have recovered from has been the obsession with weight and food. I have learned about the connection between what was going on in my life and these obsessions, and I've learned that there are better ways to deal with emotional issues. So, this story is about recovery and how I returned to a normal, balanced life.

I explore a number of treatments that helped me to overcome the disease. Some methods were traditional, some not, but they included the exploration of relationships and the importance of a solid support system. In addition, I discuss the importance of journaling, sleep and environment.

Is the book a gripping edge-of-your-seat page turner? A quick fix handy reference to recovery? No. It is a story that is real, honest and truthful.

I have written this book because I am now fully recovered. My eating disorders are over.

Inside you'll find my heart, my soul, my recovery and my gift of hope for you.

Above all, there is hope.

CONTENTS

Road to the Rainbow

ACKNOWLEDGEMENTS

This book has been in the making for years. Now, with *Road to the Rainbow* a reality, acknowledgments begin with thanks to the many colours of my life.

To my mother Betty and father Hunter, thank you for all the support, encouragement and belief in me. You never gave up. How can I possibly thank you for all that you have done? You have been behind me always on the road to my rainbow, maintaining your enthusiasm in spite of setbacks and detours. I am so glad to be able to celebrate my good health with you now.

To my brother Kingsley, for your silent strong support I will be forever grateful. To Denise, a victim of my other self, thank you for believing that wellness for me was destined to be in my future.

To Kerry, I thank you. From the day I thought I was going to die, promising me you would give my final words to my family. Thank you for your reminders of reality, times of innocence and your strength.

Also thanks to the following very special friends, some of whom have come and gone but will never be forgotten: Nicole, Pam, Alison, Jodie, Jane, Diane, Michelle, Ruth, Anne, Kim, Beth, Lisa, Nancy, Steve, Bev, Brenda, David, Koren, Maeve, Maureen, Mary, the Girouxs, BWN, Angela, Bryan, Toula, Marijke, Dorothy, Katharine, Katie and Scott.

I want to acknowledge my relationships with men and the importance of each and every one of them and their families. Were the relationships perfect? No, but I will be the first to say that I was not in the right place in my life or in my health to give a relationship all that one should. To each of them and their families, I say thank you. Particular thanks to Bill. Reading through my journals I became overwhelmed by the guilt and the pain that I put him through. I hope this book will comfort him in knowing his support was never for a moment wasted. I wish him happiness always.

I want to thank Bridget, my therapist. If there was any member of the medical fraternity who could have given up on me it was you. Thank you for never doing so.

I wish to thank Sheena's Place and its wonderful Board of Directors. I was very fortunate to have the experience as a director of this outstanding group and they give me hope that people want to help those struggling with an eating disorder, with a sensitivity that creates a home that works. Keep doing what you are doing.

Particular thanks must go to everyone at The Recorder and Times, my place of employment during most of my early years. The staff saw all the stages of my illness and I want you all to know that I have not forgotten your prayers, love and support.

Thanks to the wonderful individuals who have touched and inspired my life in very special ways like Uncle King, Twink, Wiggy, Dodo, Mac, Uncle Jack and all the special extended Grant and Ogilvie families. Thanks to Perry, not only aunt but editor several times over.

Thanks to Sue for your creativity as always, especially your contribution to this project. Also, thanks to a very wise woman, Carol.

To Paul Rabinovitch and his wife, for finding me and taking this dream to the next level, thank you.

To all of you thank you, my dream has become my reality.

Author's Note to this Edition

This book was first published in 2003 fulfilling a lifelong dream of wellness, and in putting words to paper revealed a success story of recovery. The purpose was not only to share the story of recovery but most importantly to help people struggling with this debilitating and often deadly disease.

Over the last 5 years I am heartened to know that my story has helped many to have faith and hope that wellness is indeed a reality not only for me, but for them.

As a self-published author back in 2003, copies of *Road to the Rainbow* were limited and likewise, its distribution and ability to reach many. This limitation ceased back in March of 2007 when CCB Publishing's Paul Rabinovitch and his wife caught the tail end of a television documentary done on my story of recovery and the effects on my family and friends through a program called Second Chance.

To their dismay, they had great difficulty finding a copy of my book through the regular commercial channels. Through what I deem fate, they tracked me down and proposed not only a larger distribution opportunity, and the ability to reach many sufferers, but an opportunity to update the book from then to now. My response…absolutely!

For so many reasons a revised edition spurred excitement; to let readers know not only the progress in the last five years but more importantly, that the principles I discussed in 2003 stand fast in 2008, proving yet again that what I have done indeed works. What could be more exciting than that?

So my friend, inside is the main story yet again but followed at the end of each chapter is a section entitled, "Chapter in Review". I have taken time to review journals over the last five years and have commented on life now since the initial words five years ago. You may be surprised at some of the changes; so was I, but happily so.

Over the intervening years I have spoken with people who have read the book, and the conversation has often generated several questions. The review after each chapter will now give me the opportunity to share with you some answers and perhaps shed further light on the process of recovery.

In this edition I have also provided a list of resources that have been beneficial since the book was first printed back in 2003.

For a first time reader, welcome! As my dedication reads, "I dedicate this book to you who have picked it up because you are ready to begin. Helping one person realize life is worth living has served its purpose...I hope it is you."

To those who have shared my story before, may you be comforted to know, the rainbow continues.

INTRODUCTION

I have been thinking long and hard over the last couple of years about the type of book I wanted to write. I have always known I would write one, but was never sure of the angle. That indecision is over.

With over 20 years of journals, and the documentation of the good, the bad and the ugly, I decided to dive into my recovery. As I began this process, reading my journals was often painful and pathetic. I was acutely conscious of wasted years, and occasionally I could not continue to read, but I persisted because I knew the end result would be useful not only to a sufferer, but to myself. Reviewing them was another step towards continued wellness for me.

I am not a medical professional. What I write are words from a wounded soul to a strong survivor. This book is not a medical reference book. My road to recovery may not be deemed "traditional" but it has worked for me.

My roller coaster of eating disorders has seen my 5'8" frame range from 179lbs to a mere 78lbs. With conviction stemming from experience, I empathize with all those suffering from eating disorders. I have overeaten, consuming everything in sight, hoping to numb the confusion inside. I have restricted intake hoping to literally fade away. I have dealt with the binge cycle, a short-term solution to deal with my inner pain. These latter disceses have monopolized most of my life. What I write and the feelings I note may not strike a chord for each of you, but for most, I think they will be familiar. I know the overwhelming power that food and weight can have on your life even though it is not in truth what it is all about.

Inside you will find a variety of words, diary entries, letters from family and friends, photographs, poems, quotes and journal keepsakes. I have made an effort to share the real, the raw, the results. Through my journey you will see the forks in the road and the techniques or tips that helped detour my death wish destination.

I use these techniques daily because they not only get me through my day, they help to make me enjoy my day.

Sounds impossible doesn't it?

If you are as I was, you could not imagine looking forward to the morning. The dread, the weigh scale, the food, the clothes, the social functions, the people, the comments; it was a battle to deal with every day, every hour, every minute, every second.

It is important to note that what works for me may not work for you. The idea is to adapt the ideas that best work for you. The suggestions in this book are meant to initiate change and stimulate a new thought process for you towards wellness. It will take a lot of practice to change. One phrase that has real merit is, "fake it 'til you feel it." Over time you will be amazed by the change.

I have agonized on the format knowing that I have suffered from a wide range of eating disorders, but that feeling vanished after I attended a recent book reading. The author who had written her own painful life story advised me to "Dig in. Go with your heart. The rest will take care of itself." So inside..... is my heart.

I hope you enjoy this book. Its aim is to inform, provoke, but most importantly to inspire you to take that first step in recovery. You are worth the effort.

Journal Entry
February 21st 1993

> *You cannot climb high mountains*
> *Before you've walked low ground*
> *And on the road to wisdom*
> *No short cuts can be found*
> *Have courage in adversity*
> *You will not strive in vain*
> *There never was a rainbow*
> *Without a fall of rain.*

I wish I had written the name of the author of this poem but to whoever it is, thank you. I wrote down this poem as I was struggling one day with how to get better, not understanding the painful process. And it is a process, not a quick fix.

As I read through my journals it is hard to believe the person's handwriting was mine, that the deep thoughts, the pain, the suffering were mine. The hatred, the self loathing, the paranoia, the jealousy, the meanness, the feelings were all mine.

The hollowness, the cold and stinging hands, the swollen legs, the longing for death. Every feeling, every desperate thought...mine!

Who was that person?

Today I embrace life, participate in life, look forward to life!

How can I possibly be the same person? I look at pictures and I seemed so sad, so numb and now it's as though I have had life pumped back into me. I wish the way I feel now was contagious because I'd fill a room with eating disorder sufferers and spread it endlessly. But it's not that simple. The disease is never the same for two and neither is recovery, but stories can be shared.

"I believe that the element of sharing stories of wellness is crucial for recovery. When we tell our stories, even if for a moment, isolation is gone. Sharing the pain and the struggle seems to lessen the bad thoughts and sharing stories of recovery reminds us and encourages us to continue trying."

Maybe there is one thing in someone's story that you have not heard or tried. It may be the something that can make a difference for you. I have chosen to write this book because I am well and want to share my road to the rainbow with others, hoping that something I have done can help you. My aim is to help many, but my soul will be filled if one person can be helped because it begins with one. One drop to begin an ocean; one brick to build a museum; one step on the road; one step towards the rainbow.

I begin this book with painful and dark journal entries. I want to share them because I feel it is important to understand the rain, in order to appreciate the rainbow. It is important to know where I have been: the journey from the depths of despair to a life filled with the colours of the rainbow, a life filled with joy, contentment, calm, peace and enthusiasm.

Maybe some of these feelings will hit a nerve, I hope they do. I let you in, to let you know, you are not alone.

Journal Entry
April 5th 1989
        "Publisher's daughter found dead in Garage –
Suicide Suspected"

Local publisher of The Recorder and Times, Hunter Grant, has lost his daughter late yesterday afternoon due to apparent suicide. Meredith Grant was found dead this afternoon by Steve Hook who, simply going to the house to visit, noticed an exhaust smell coming from the garage. Hook entered the garage to find the engine of the 1987 Tercel on with Miss Grant inside, door locked.

Police and ambulance were notified and Miss Grant was pronounced dead on arrival. Hunter Grant and his wife Betty were notified immediately in Toronto where they were both attending a Newspaper conference. Both in shock, they arrived home late last evening and are concentrating on arrangements to be made.

Meredith 23, was born in Brockville August 7th, 1965. She attended Brock and Prince of Wales Public Schools, Grenville Christian College, completed high school at Brockville Collegiate Institute, and received a BA from Wilfrid Laurier University. Meredith was known for her involvement in school activities, over the years playing basketball, volleyball, and was on the sports banquet and graduation committee as well as students council. She was known as an organizer.

In June Meredith was accepted with the international group Up With People travelling through much of the US and Europe but due to failing health was forced to leave the program in January. She was involved in the community with Big Sisters and worked for the family business starting at the age of 13. Surviving are father and mother Hunter and Betty Grant (Brockville) and brother Kingsley Grant (Whitehorse). Funeral services will be set for Sunday.

Pall bearers are Steve Hook, Scott Giroux, Craig Brown, Joe Haggett and Bob Anderson. Charitable donations to a cause of your choice would be greatly appreciated.

Reflection 2001

What to say? Writing my own obituary. Sad. I can't believe I felt so desperate although I remember the entry. So much has happened since then; so much life and so much wellness. I am glad this wished destiny did not become my fate. It's odd because while I mention an illness, I did not acknowledge the illness as an eating disorder. I denied it for a very long time. I felt depressed all the time, numb as though nothing would ever get better. I look back on my life then and people used to say, "You have so much to live for, to be grateful for." I couldn't see it. I did not realize at that time that being malnourished could affect how I thought or perceived things. It has since become crystal clear.

Today I cannot imagine writing my obituary. My parents are well, and my relationship with both is amazing. My brother is happily married and has given our family the gift of two very special people: Hunter and Walker. Life since that date has been filled with memories, and had I died I would not have experienced the joy our family feels today.

Today, I don't fight life, I embrace it.

It's wonderful.

Journal Entry

November 7th 1992

I saw Steve (family physician) yesterday and my weight was down; while a part of me was quite surprised another said, "Good." It's like there was this

11

voice inside of me that whispered, "That's what you should weigh," and then even another voice was angry and so frustrated. I want to beat this so badly. It's as though if I could only "see it" and then fight it, but it's an enigma: one that I can't see, hold, feel or touch. It truly is unreal and a distortion.

I get so angry at myself for putting myself here, it's as though I'm trapped in this thinning mask.

Journal Entry
December 9th 1992

Oh to live a normal life, perhaps for me it is too demanding a request to wish for. Bottom line I probably don't deserve it. Often I seriously wish I was dead. I so often feel more like a nuisance more than anything else. When I feel like this I usually just shut things off, it's easier to be numb than to be alert.

Look at the people in Somalia, who get nothing, the sick thing is I like the way they look, plus it stresses the fact to me that I could easily be thinner than I am. I feel so intensely ugly and repulsive.

Words that describe me: don't fit, ugly and fat, greedy, hurting, worthless, lonely, gross, disgusting, confused, sad, screwed up, numb, nervous and young.

January 12, 2002

Today I sit with over 20 years worth of journal entries that have particular significance, ones that I feel may be of help to others and serve as the foundation of this book. Most of the entries are along the same vein as the ones you have already read. Do I continue with journal entries? I will be honest that I really am not sure where to start. My road to the rainbow has not been as easy as 1+1=2.

Today I reviewed some photographs with my parents, and I could tell how painful it was for all of us to look back on them. It also made me realize yet again the importance of my recovery not only to me but to my family. My life is back, and so is theirs. Even 5 years ago my time with them on vacation would have been dictated by a weigh scale. Today the vacation is filled with wonderful conversation, much laughter, much health and the end result of never having enough hours in the day to do all that needs to be done.

How did I get to this place of health?

Let me tell you first where I have been.

INTRODUCTION IN REVIEW

As I reviewed my words in the introduction I am aware of its simplicity and have been asked why I did not expand on the disease or painful journal entries? A very simple response: a sufferer knows all too well the pain and need not be reminded.

I also have a personal view that sharing too many details on the disease can actually have damaging effects to the reader. Rather than help, it can actually encourage the disease by providing details of how you continued your behaviour. Sufferers will do anything to hold on to the disease, and at all times, on the hunt for any new trick that could possibly improve the end result.

How can that be?

An eating disorder sufferer's mind is much different than that of a non-sufferer. A non-sufferer may believe that to read the behaviour in detail would be a deterrent to starting the behaviour. Ironically for the sufferer, it enhances it. I know how the mind of an eating disorder sufferer works, thus details are left to a minimum. This book is about recovery from the disease, not the disease itself.

CHAPTER ONE

The Pain, The Past

Often people ask, "What made you get or have an eating disorder?" Each person has a different story as to how their eating disorder developed or progressed, which I believe adds to the difficulty in helping those suffering from the disease. For some it is peer pressure or media influence or athletics, but for others it can be a way of coping with abuse: physical, sexual or emotional. Also, divorce or death of a parent, or the breakdown of a relationship can be the catalyst; the list is long. But for sure, an eating disorder stems from something deeper than weight and food. The preoccupation with weight and food are a symptom of other issues.

My first issue was abuse.

I remember being a happy although sensitive kid. My life changed when I was 10 and babysat for a neighbour. I remember feeling very uncomfortable around the father and that he used to touch me in places where I had never been touched before. His words and messages were damaging to me. They killed my self esteem when I was too young to know better. During flashbacks in adulthood, I remembered being told by this neighbour that I was fat and ugly and that anyone of any worth would have nothing to do with me. He became mad at me if I ate anything at their house. I recall him putting my head in the toilet making me be sick to get rid of it. It was a horrible and painful memory to relive but the memories have shed light on my thoughts and subsequent behaviour as I was growing up.

The abuse happened in an era when such things were not discussed, and as a result I kept the abuse a secret until I was 21 years old. Time has allowed me to deal with this issue, but in reality it served as the onset of my eating disorder. The abuse changed how I felt about myself and influenced future relationships for years. The abuse became the root; it grabbed hold. The thoughts and feelings that had developed during the abuse continued to be reinforced.

During the time of my abuse I was a "chubby" child, as I recall being called. I used food as a comfort and used it to cover over my pain. From this time until the end of high school I used food as a way to numb the pain. Other pressures were evident: peer pressure, comments and jokes from boys. In grade 5, I was chased down the street after school by a couple of the popular boys at school who called me Bessie the Cow. I was devastated. I remember thinking maybe my abuser was right. These boys were reinforcing the thoughts that had already been firmly placed in my mind.

Preoccupation with food and weight at this time was also emerging within my family. My dad had been told by his doctor to lose weight and he heeded his advice immediately, seeming to live off half a grapefruit and chilled consommé.

There is such irony about weight. It is not healthy to weigh too much, but it is equally as life threatening to weigh too little. Unfortunately Dad's eating behaviour and the knowledge he was gaining about food, weight, cholesterol, etc., became information that was shared with us as well, in excess. Dad will be the first to acknowledge hounding us on our eating habits. As a family, we have been able to discuss this influence and how important a support system is, not only in recovery, but its influence in how you perceive yourself.

16

"A parent's or caretaker's view of him/herself, and views towards food, exercise and body image can have a huge impact on a child."

Messages of losing weight were also reinforced by the diet books and quick fix diets plastered on magazine covers picked up by Mom at the local grocery store. My mother was not alone in these purchases. Most of my friends' mothers had the same magazines on their coffee tables. Also, as early as elementary school the "girls" envied the stars and the shapes they portrayed on the pages of magazines and on television screens.

Within our family, weight issues were a concern of more than one relative. I remember going to my grandmother's and diet pills were everywhere. My aunts talked about the battle of the bulge. It was pervasive.

It certainly was not my parent's intent to encourage an eating disorder. In my father's case he was following doctor's orders and in my mother's case, influenced by media messages and her own personal environment. As my dad always said, "You don't go to school to be a parent," and parents certainly have not been well informed on eating disorders. The shame of it is that often parents have to learn about eating disorders long after symptoms are recognized, instead of having the information as a proactive device earlier on.

The truth is that we are bombarded with messages about food and weight. We are obsessed with cooking shows and recipes, but at the same time encouraged to limit intake and join one weight program after the other...mixed messages? I certainly think so. You can watch a program with celebrity chefs like Wolfgang Puck creating a cheese dish and the commercial following the program is a Weight Watchers promotional ad.

And so a trend developed. Through therapy, journaling and education I began to see that while low self esteem was firmly rooted, continuing circumstances reinforced those ingrained messages.

I have often said throughout my recovery, "Give me any other problem with a substance," for example, cigarettes. In truth, your body does not need nicotine to remain alive but it does require food, so you must learn how to deal with it. The reality is food serves a variety of purposes beyond nutrition. In food, people find comfort. They use it as a reward. It's a hobby for others, a recreation. But also to many, food is an enemy. The trick is appreciating it for what it is...fuel. I have said to students, "Think of it like gas in a car: too little it won't move; too much it overflows." For all of us it means finding a happy medium. For an eating disorder sufferer this happy medium often seems elusive, but it is possible.

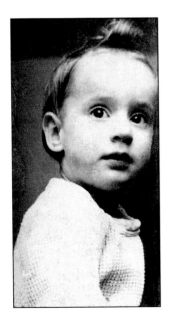

The innocence of the child.
Meredith around 2 years old.

*The innocence taken away.
10 years old... abuse beginning.*

*Increase in weight,
using food as a comfort.*

The Past Continues.....

While the abuse triggered the development of an eating disorder, emotional issues also escalated the problem.

In grade 9 I attended a private school with very bizarre practices which continued to complicate my problem. Before I stepped in the door of this establishment I had low self esteem. Having been abused, I was emotional and vulnerable. Unfortunately, while not planned, the school became yet another reinforcement of low self esteem.

Three episodes in particular were notable. The first was during a Bible class with all the female boarders. The headmaster's wife read a scripture dealing with men and women, with the message that any intimacy prior to marriage was a sin. I thought, "Not only do I feel odd to begin with having been touched and treated inappropriately by a neighbour, but now in the eyes of God I am considered a sinner too."

The reinforcements continued. During a communion service I fell asleep and one of the girls said she wanted to talk to me with the "ladies" after chapel. I remember three staff members and this girl saying they felt a bad spirit from me in church and that I needed to ask the lord to show me where I was wrong. Everything was always my fault. I wasn't even allowed to be tired. The influence and the mind bending tricks by the ladies continued. I recall being awakened by one of the "ladies" (this is the phrase given to the female staff) very late in the evening (I had been asleep for some time). I was brought into a room where all the female staff were waiting. I remember thinking how it was extremely odd that one was ironing while the remainder of them sat in a circle on chairs. What was going on? I soon found out.

I was put in the middle of this circle. One by one they

insulted me, said I had a bad spirit, and that I was a rotten apple spoiling the barrel. They asked if I knew what my problem was? I answered no. They went on to discuss their theory... my problem was that my father loved my brother, and he didn't love me.

What kind of sick people do this? I certainly did not think God-fearing Christians did. Over the years I have learned not to equate all Christians with this group and thankfully redeveloped my faith. The sad thing about this incident is that I believed them for many years thereafter. It was another thought that was wrongly enforced on me that continued to grow. I was only 14 years old. I was feeling so confused and cornered by these adults. I felt as though I had little or no control over anything, including my feelings.

I decided to go on a hunger strike, eating nothing, and I lost 20lbs in a little over two weeks. I was driving the staff nuts and it became a tool for getting me out of the school as a boarder. I was being heard; I had power; I had control.

Things seemed to settle down for a while when I returned to the local high school with familiar friends and a happy environment, but deep down I still felt sad and overwhelmed by the feelings I had inside. I had particular difficulty with relationships, especially in terms of intimacy. I began to overeat, initially to comfort myself, and ballooned to 178lbs (the first of many unhealthy weights). I didn't feel any better at this weight and I was out of control: not only was my weight out of control, but also my life. I asked myself if I had ever felt in control. If only for a brief moment I did remember sensing control when I lost weight. It began again. But this time it was different.

I began with losing a few pounds, looking and feeling better and trying any diet that would hasten results. Positive comments began, and I felt good, but food was always around and I began a love/hate relationship with it. On the one hand, I had used it for comfort to the point of excess and on the other, it became an enemy. As I continued to lose weight and the number on the weigh scale continued to decline, it became a game, and an aspect of control I had never sensed before. With all the things that had happened and the feelings I had hidden inside, the need for control became intense.

I think it is important to note that this need for control and the loss of weight were happening at a time when I still had not told anyone about my childhood experiences. Also, the loss of weight and this element of total control were becoming euphoric. I thought about nothing other than the scale and losing more and more weight. It didn't matter what happened in my life. All the things that I couldn't control became comforted by what I could...my weight.

While at university my disordered eating became serious towards the end of my time there. The need to succeed, finishing something, became another pressure. To do well wasn't good enough. The already obsessive thoughts of having to be perfect, everything right, were full steam ahead. The weight continued to drop and if I had to eat anything that was not planned I went into a rage. My first attempt at suicide took place during this time. I had never been that sick and it had surprisingly gratifying results...I had lost 10 more pounds. But while the weight continued to fall off, my self loathing continued and increased. I was beginning a life of self torture.

I completed university which was a huge accomplishment for me. Then, within a year, I was on my way to Tucson, Arizona to perform with the entertainment group Up with People. This group continued to reinforce the body image that was becoming ingrained in my mind. Since a high priority was put on looks, presentation and the entertainment value, it became yet again an issue that could not be avoided. I remember girls being pulled from lead roles because they were too heavy. They were devastated and it just made me want to continue keeping control. It became another reason to keep on doing what I was doing. I was down to eating only an apple a day.

The control became insane. I don't know when I crossed the line. All I know is that journals were no longer chronicles of life but rather pages and pages of weight entries, calorie intake, exercise, calories burned, days planned around how I would avoid situations with food, and if I had to eat, how I would get rid of it.

I have read through years and years of these journal entries. Moments of euphoria were noted if I had lost weight and hours of anxiety if I had not. I look back on those entries and acknowledge that there were no feelings, no thoughts, no emotions...just numbers and more numbers.

As we toured, while staying with host families I would immediately go to the bathroom to find a scale. In Europe, I had to convert kilograms to pounds, so a calculator was in order. But what was happening, even though I couldn't see it at the time, was that my low body weight resulted in poor judgement and irrational thoughts. I was becoming very depressed. During Christmas break, my boyfriend of seven years broke up with me at 12:50 on New Year's Eve. My depression reached a critical level. I returned to Up with People in the US in January. During a stay in Hattiesburg Mississippi, I took every pill in my host family's medicine cabinet in my second attempt to kill myself. I was very ill, but death escaped me again.

Lisa, a dear friend in the cast became my rock. We were in New Orleans for a two-hour stay until we headed to our next overnight city, Mobile, Alabama. I told her I just didn't think I was going to make it. I was so depressed. I told her what had happened. I said there was something very wrong that despite this wonderful opportunity to travel, I felt nothing.

I remember calling my parents from a payphone in Mobile. I told my dad that I had to come home; if I didn't now, I never would. He was great. He said that I was to book a ticket and he and Mom would pick me up in Syracuse, New York. I asked them not to ask questions when they picked me up. I vaguely remember the pick up. I felt numb. The disease had grabbed hold.

When I arrived home I saw a therapist, but because she was a family friend it was not the right fit. I then began seeing Bridget and continued to do so for years. During this time, my mom and I went for a walk in the pines, a wooded area west of our home, and she was struggling as a mother to understand what was going on. Why did I have such self loathing? I had so much to live for...why couldn't I see that? This is when I finally told her about the abuse. I have never seen my mother so distraught. Did it feel better to tell her? Yes, but at the same time, due to my malnourishment and inability to look at a situation rationally, I thought it was the wrong thing to do because now it had hurt Mom. Can you see how the cycle gets so twisted?

My parents were more than willing to take action against my abuser and perhaps others would have done so, but I decided to leave it alone. I did not want to relive it again. The thing that seemed to be most important to me was getting that information out. This became the beginning of an outpouring of emotion. The struggle to do so continued for another ten painful years.

And it got worse before it got better.

I continued to work and ran on adrenaline. I seemed to be able to keep up with deadlines and actually excel in my projects. It was as if work and the disease were an all consuming preoccupation in my life (even though I denied the problem). The insanity continued; it was as though there was a sense within me that life was destined to be short. I was feeling so many things. The eating disorder already had its grip on me when I told my family about the abuse. Perhaps things might have been different if I had been able to talk about the abuse years earlier. I will never know, but I think if I had discussed it then, expressed myself in a healthy manner, the horrible journey through eating disorders may have been derailed.

> ***"I believe the element of being able to express yourself is key to avoiding the onset of an eating disorder as well as avoiding a relapse in recovery."***

I will continue to reinforce this element of expression throughout the book.

The next few years saw the continuation of weight loss. The grip of anorexia was strong during this time. I was married in 1990 to Bill, a true angel. He did more than try to help and support me through this struggle but the disease was overwhelming...stronger than either of us would know.

My weight dropped and dropped to the lowest point of 78 lbs on this 5'8" frame of mine. Over the years I had been hospitalized on several occasions while always insisting that I didn't have a problem...that I was fine. I couldn't see then what I see now: the importance of nutrition not only for my body but for my mind. Not only had I lost weight. I had in the process lost my self, my soul and my spirit. I had lost my sense of reality. I became paranoid, hypersensitive to criticism, and I hurt. I hurt all over. I lost myself to the point that I just wanted to die, to have it all over with because to let go of this control would be too overwhelming to bear. To gain a pound meant I had failed, that I was no longer good at one thing.

I wouldn't... more importantly... I couldn't let go.

I wanted to be thinner and thinner, in hopes of eventually disappearing. A part of me took pride in my achievement. I had always considered myself mediocre, not good at anything. I finally found something I was good at...really good at.

I continued to flip through magazines as many of us do. I would continue to make sure I could feel my ribs and get my thumb and first finger around my arm. I would constantly measure my waist, my thighs, and top off the process with a step on the scale. I would see others who I deemed thinner than I and would write that I still had a long way to go before I was that thin. I think there is a bizarre envy that women have towards other women who seem to have controlled their weight, particularly when you have an eating disorder. In August of 1993 I received a letter from an anonymous young woman in the town in which I lived, who was also an eating disorder sufferer. Perhaps what was most unsettling about the letter was the following:

"I thought maybe it would make me feel better to write to you and tell you that I admire your willpower and strength to continue being as thin as you are. Every time I see you I feel envious of that power and it scares me because I want it."

There is something very different with respect to perception when you are suffering from an eating disorder. When you get into this "headspace", it becomes a language all its own and to break through is one hell of a difficult task. Everything took a second seat to my disease: my relationship, my family, friends and ultimately, my work.

Over the next few years, I was in and out of hospitals with my health continuing to deteriorate along with almost all my relationships. My menstrual cycle had stopped years before. I was emaciated and constantly cold. My skin was a pasty colour. My electrolytes were out of whack; potassium levels low, teeth deteriorating, and muscle spasms beginning. Emotionally I was lethargic, extremely irritable and easily frustrated. The need for perfection was intense. The self torture was insane and it affected everything and everyone around me.

How did I get better? It did not happen overnight but instead was a lengthy road to a life I now call the rainbow. Throughout my journals, a number of things reappeared that were good. They helped make it a better day, and with patience and time, a better life. My hope is that the information I share with you will help you too.

Hovering around 80 lbs.

1990 Honeymoon in Florida

1991 – 93 lbs.: Smiles... but everyday a struggle.

One of a few hospital stays.

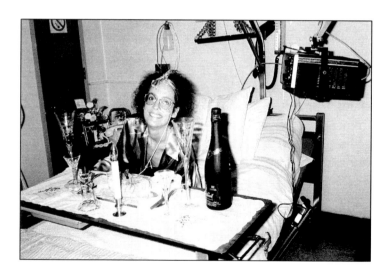

Ringing in the New Year... a wonderful location.

CHAPTER ONE IN REVIEW

It is amazing how life, when you let it, does indeed fall into place and come full circle. With it, constant changes, and what I know now is a constant process. Today with wellness those changes are manageable. I see so clearly now that the key to dealing with change is being balanced mentally, physically and emotionally.

Upon reviewing Chapter One, "The Pain the Past", I am reminded just how the life process works. I discussed a few of the issues that served as a catalyst for my disease: sexual and emotional abuse, family dynamics, peer pressure and the media.

Still today the media continues to promote the perfect body and at the same time discusses the issue of eating disorders to a degree never seen before. It is strangely becoming the "in thing" to have. Each week another tabloid is exploiting another young actress as she struggles to survive in the public jungle, coping by shedding pounds. While the exposure to the disease's issues is a good thing, the fame they are attaching to it is not. At the same time, one of the top rated television programs presently is "The Biggest Loser".

What I have come to realize with all the exposure to weight issues, be it the obesity epidemic in North America or the danger of eating disorders, is that the news is not going to disappear. My recovery and the personal work I continue to do allow me to filter out this information, putting it where it needs to be without affecting me personally. I encourage those embracing the road to recovery to do the same.

I've been asked by readers, "Do the old messages ever go away?" The question often being asked is in reference to my sexual abuse by a neighbour, and the emotional abuse by members of the clergy at the private school I attended in high school. My answer is…the messages never go away completely but with wellness I have been able to process them in a way that they no longer influence my day to day activities.

That's what recovery allows you to do; realistically put things where they need to be placed within your life's history. What you ultimately realize is that you can choose to stay in the past and the negativity that's attached to it, or you can deal with the present, the now and move on. This aspect of being 100% present in the now has been key to how I live my life today.

Initially, eating disorders were how I coped with those messages, and being too afraid to let go of what worked, I continued my downward spiral. An eating disorder did not resolve my past or help deal with the pain I felt; conversely, it prolonged the pain and suffering.

With all the techniques I discussed in the first edition of the book, communicating my feelings, proper sleep, nutrition and physical activity, and a positive environment, I know this is indeed the healthy way to cope with my past history. I have learned through exploring my feelings that there is healing and most importantly there is life.

I am reminded of a great Cherokee story *The Two Wolves Within*; it illustrates my point of negative versus positive better than anything I have ever read before…

The Cherokee (Tsalagi) Nation believed that within each person was a battle between two wolves. Sitting with his grandson, a grandfather explained that one of the wolves was evil and was driven by anger, envy, sorrow, regret, greed, arrogance, self-pity, guilt, resentment, inferiority, lies, false pride, superiority and ego.

The other wolf was good, and was driven by joy, peace, love, hope, serenity, humility, kindness, benevolence, empathy, generosity, truth, compassion and faith.

Thinking about the wolves already growing within him, the boy asked, "Grandfather, which wolf wins?"

And the old Cherokee simply replied, "The one you feed."

Our mind is such a powerful thing; it has the power to see life in light or in darkness, in peace or in chaos, balance or mayhem. The key is to pick the positive. While life can toss us challenges each day, we are given choices, and recovery allows the choices to be made with a clear head.

I will be honest and let you know that unfortunately there are days when you will feed the wrong wolf. What I have learned, and probably more so since first writing the book, is to take those days as a sign to discover what is troubling you. What do you need to address? What do you need to say? Having survived an eating disorder myself, in a way I am somehow more in tune to trouble within and the need to address the trouble. Of course it is not always easy to confront the trouble, but in the long run it will become clear that it is not only the better option but the only option.

I have also learned that given time, certain life challenges have a remarkable way of working themselves out. If you are true to yourself and your soul things will work out in the long run; they usually do.

When discussing my past in this chapter I mentioned a devastating experience at a private school during my high school years and the damage done psychologically and emotionally during that time. In the summer of 2007 the school shut its doors and shortly after a number of investigations began. As I write this, a criminal investigation by the Ontario Provincial Police (OPP) and several lawsuits are in progress.

I must be honest with you that those old feelings raised their head, the hurt, the anger, the rage and I was afraid. I was afraid that they were going to get away with closing their doors and the truth would be buried forever. I remember going for a run the next morning with tears in my eyes, yelling what do I do? I listened to my heart, to my soul and it said to wait. It will look after itself, the story will be told. A few weeks later a national newspaper here in Canada, The Globe and Mail, broke the story of abuse.

I was overwhelmed with the past, and the memories that went along with it; even now as I write this the feelings are real and present, but with wellness they are in perspective. It doesn't mean that there's no coping process but the eating disorder behaviours are no longer that option. It is now about speaking out publicly and privately, and knowing it is not only okay, but my right.

I won't lie to you, life's memories and life's challenges and dealing with them are not easy. But, it is life. Recovery doesn't mean that you won't have a bad day, or a huge question mark as to your place on this earth, but it will pass. I think if there is anything that I have learned since first writing this book is that to think that life will be perfect or trying to keep things perfect is a huge mistake. You need to be realistic with life's happenings and its changes and let them flow naturally, as naturally as you take a breath.

Keep the course, and as my mom has always said, "Go where the love is," to pass the hurdle. And learn, take the bad moment and learn. We all know about triggers, and they are equally important to be aware of during our recovery. With every struggle comes a lesson, an invaluable one. As Wayne Dyer says in his book *Change Your Thoughts, Change Your Life, Living the Wisdom of the Tao*, "Nature doesn't create a storm that never ends. Within misfortune, good fortune hides."

CHAPTER TWO

The Beginning of the Rainbow
Admission, Honesty and Attitude
Where Recovery Begins

As anyone who has suffered from an eating disorder will agree, "Admitting you have a problem is the first step," is a phrase you have heard often. But there is a real difference between admitting you have a problem and wanting to get better. For years I denied I had a problem, but once I did, I quickly learned admission is just the first step. Admission alone does not make one well.

I talk about honesty and attitude throughout this book because of their importance. My road to the rainbow was often sidetracked due to my dishonesty and negative attitude. I now know how important choosing to be positive is to recovery.

Once I admitted the problem, I continued to look for a quick fix. Throughout recovery, I had to come to grips with the crucial fact that this was not going to happen overnight. I learned the importance of being thankful for 5 seconds (let alone 5 minutes) when I lacked obsession, didn't weigh myself or calculate the fat grams in a slice of cheese. If something happened and I had a relapse, I needed to appreciate that the important thing was learning about the relapse: What was going on? What was the trigger? What was happening? What was I feeling? Why couldn't I express myself?

Looking at the day as a good 5 minutes, 5 more than I had yesterday, worked for me. Looking at the glass half full, not half empty became increasingly important. My parents used this phrase constantly. I had to learn it myself. It was a positive message continually reinforced within my family and I am extremely grateful.

I cannot tell you how important it is to avoid being self deprecating. You need to shake the "I will never get better" mindset. How do you do that? Practice! Say to yourself "Yes I can" and "I will get better" and keep saying it over and over again. Get on the horse and give it another shot, remember... you are worth the effort! I still positively talk to myself everyday. I continually reinforce the positive about what is going on and it is amazing to feel the difference in energy. Do I lean on others at times for that added positive support? Absolutely! I am human and, for example, now that I have a regular period once again, emotional changes occur and I tend to get weepy and a little down in the dumps. I continue with the positive talk but will call a member of my family or a friend for support. I don't have to get through those moments alone and neither do you.

One important thing I have learned regarding keeping my attitude in check is not to take on someone else's feelings or attitude. For example, recently I met a woman who seemed unfriendly. In the past, I would have thought there was something wrong with me, or that I had done something wrong. I make every attempt now not to take on the feelings of others. They own them. I don't.

Something that continues to be of tremendous support to me and to my attitude are quotes to start the day. Every morning I read a quote from a variety of books: some on motivation, others on attitude. Which reference book you use is up to you. Each week I put a quote on my answering machine to kick off the week. They not only help me, but tend to be thought provoking for the caller. Friends have often told me that hearing the quote influenced their day and helped them out. Quotes have helped me to stay focused and on track with a positive attitude and outlook towards each day.

Following are a few quotes that I have noted in my journals and have been of particular support to me over the years. I have tried to note the source, but often, when I found them, they were not noted. I acknowledge them all, known and unknown and say thanks for these inspiring messages.

I recommend that you keep this list close by. The quote you choose to read in the morning may be the one to help you get through the moment. And remember, the moments add up to a day. For me it was uncanny how appropriate the quote was for the day.

Quotes to help through recovery

"Worrying costs much and accomplishes little"

"I see others clearly only when I see myself clearly"

"Never give up then, for that is just the place and time that the tide will turn"

"No one can make you feel inferior without your consent"
- Eleanor Roosevelt

"Character contributes to beauty a mode of conduct, a standard of courage, discipline, fortitude, and integrity can do a great deal to make a woman beautiful"
- Jacqueline Bisset

"I am what I am. To look for reasons is beyond the point"
- Joan Didion

"The brightest future will always be based on a forgotten past. You can't go on well in life until you let go of your past failures and heartaches"

"Perspective I soon realized was a fine commodity, but utterly useless when I was in the thick of things"
- Ingrid Bergis

"The key is to keep company only with people who uplift you, whose presence calls forth your best"
- Epictetus

"If you wait till you're ready you won't do anything"

"The only limits I have are those I place on myself"

"You don't have to look any farther for a helping hand than the end of your arm"

"Peace is when time doesn't matter when it passes by"

"An optimist is one who takes cold water thrown upon his idea, heats it with enthusiasm and uses the steam to push ahead"

"Do not go where the path may lead, instead go where there is no path and leave a trail"

"It isn't until you come to a spiritual understanding of who you are; not necessarily a religious feeling, but deep down the spirit within, that you can begin to take control"
- Oprah Winfrey

"If you do not tell the truth about yourself you cannot tell it about other people"
- Virginia Woolf

"A self-centered perspective takes more from me than it brings to me"

"You gain strength, courage, and confidence by every experience in which you really stop to look fear in the face"
- Eleanor Roosevelt

"In the midst of winter I finally learned that there was in me an invincible summer"
- Albert Camus

"All glory comes from daring to begin"

"You cannot hurt your eyesight by looking on the bright side"

"A father is not someone to lean on but who makes leaning unnecessary"

"It is never too late to be what you might have been"
- George Eliot

"Let the world know you as you are, not as you think you should be"

"Give the world all that you have, and the best will come back to you"
- Madeline Bridges

"Everything has its wonders, even darkness and silence, and I learn whatever state I may be in, there in to be content"
- Helen Keller

"A thought is merely a suggestion, it isn't a command."
- Linda Crawford

"Look back but don't stare. It is only when I make peace with what is behind me that I set my sights on what's ahead."

"You cannot give to or love another until you love yourself."
- My wonderful mother

I believe that the moment we each want to get better is a moving target, never the same for any two people. For some it is hitting rock bottom, often more than once. For others it need not go that far, but however we get there, the road ahead looks daunting indeed and for me the above quotes have helped.

The issue of honesty in relation to recovery is often difficult to face. For many years I hid my disease and my habits. I avoided and lied to myself, everyone around me, co-workers, friends and my family. I said what they wanted to hear, said how much better I was doing, allowing the lies to continue. I have learned that honesty in the long run is better for everyone. Over the years, I have been able to candidly discuss my illness and I quickly learned that all the years I thought I was covering up in fact fooled no one. I was just too stubborn to be stopped.

Relationships were lost because of my illness and my dishonesty. There have been regrets and much guilt surrounding relationships, but in order to move on, I have had to put those losses in perspective. I have learned to appreciate the importance each has had and will always have in my life, while understanding that in order for me to have reached this state of wellness, they are not meant to be part of my life now. One thing I have realized over the years is that it is extremely difficult to have healthy relationships when you are not healthy. Relationships are difficult at the best of times, and when you are well, relationships have a stronger chance of surviving.

An important element in my eating disorder recovery was forgiving myself and apologizing for the pain I had caused others. I truly believe the road to my rainbow would have been far more difficult had I not done that.

I had to forgive myself in order to move on. Forgive myself for events and opportunities missed. Forgive myself for inappropriate decisions and behaviour. I knew what they were. I kept all the details in my journals. In most cases the behaviour and attitude affected other people and other lives and acknowledging them and asking for forgiveness was key. I could not take back the past, but I was in a position to improve upon the future.

In some cases the apologies were made face to face, some by phone, others through letters. Often those I needed to apologize to said it was not necessary. I insisted that it was and needed to hear from them whether the apology was accepted or not. As well, letters were sent. In some cases no response. For those to whom I have not heard back, I continue to be comforted by the fact that I know that I have sent them my thoughts and feelings. This step is an important cleansing, so crucial for me to work through the recovery process.

For some of you apologies may not be in order but honest real talk is. Maybe you need to talk to family members about your feelings, about what you're going through. You cannot expect family, friends and professionals to understand, and they will have no idea unless you speak to them and tell the truth. In my case, it was best to talk to a therapist first about what to say to those people. This gives you a chance to role play and go through the motions first. I will be talking about therapy later on.

Attitude

There is a reason why there are shelves and shelves of self help books at your local bookstore; they help people. Knowing that I had to try to get better, I turned everywhere for anything that would help. There were many I was given, several bought, but one in particular that is worth noting is Gary Zukav's, *Seat of the Soul*.

Why this book specifically?

Often I wrote in my journal about my purpose, me as a person, and that surely I could not be going through this disease without a reason. The pain I felt had to have a purpose, and as sick as I got there was always something within me that said I indeed had a purpose, a reason for being, that was bigger than my illness. The disease covered or layered who I was, what I was meant to be and do.

Ironically Mr. Zukav equates this soul searching with a hunger and in doing so seemed to relate to what I was feeling even more. It was that filling of a void that I could relate to. Whether I was in an anorexic or a bulimic thought/behaviour mode they were performed with the intent of filling some void. The thoughts and behaviours were for whatever reason filling that void. What Mr. Zukav's book made me realize was that with the behaviour, these addictions, are serving a purpose. They mask and detain someone from being real, being well, being happy. They are a cover up and a waste of energy for the soul. It is when we are willing to be honest and truthful with ourselves that wellness starts. It is changing one's attitude, changing the mindset. Best to challenge the old and bring in the new.

To a well person, Mr. Zukav's book reinforced for me the fact that once you acknowledge and accept your realities and make an attempt to move beyond them, your soul, your personality, who you really are, rises to the surface and real life begins.

It is at this place that you can face the reality of what your soul is meant to do. While I was in the crisis of my disease, I felt numb to life, to a purpose. The disease, as I mentioned before, nicely covered it. Very often I did things to please others, things I thought they wanted me to do. It became a part of the cycle. Instead of being honest with what I needed, I allowed my needs to take a back seat and continuing my eating disorder(s), and it became my way of coping instead of confronting the truth about what I needed, felt and thought. What made things more difficult was the fact that I did not know what I wanted to do. This book in particular made me realize that to continue with my negative patterns was going to keep me forever at arm's length from my own soul's purpose. A quote I'm reminded of is, *"Keep doing what you've always done and you'll get what you've always gotten."*

For me, one of the important messages about Zukav's book was that we all have a purpose and we should expose that purpose, not hide it. When you go with that soul, that gut feeling, or intuition, things fall into place. Along with this sentiment is also the importance of positive thought and behaviour. I say this because I have tried it and it works. The healthier I became, the better able I was to see and feel the real me. I realized that being malnourished was robbing my soul. Meredith was slipping and fading away in all aspects of my life. It is amazing that as I nourished my body, I was nourishing my mind, spirit and soul as well. When you are being your real self, you are buoyant. I have also learned the truth that if you radiate illness, pessimism, sadness, fear and suspicion then that is indeed what you receive in return.

Seat of the Soul taught me that the more you challenge a negative force, the more it loses its power. For me, the eating disorder and its power were in control, and I had to face it and fight it. This element of fight reminded me of a phrase from my father during the throes of my illness, "Mer, you have an angel on one shoulder and a devil on the other. You are letting the devil win by listening to him." When I was very ill, it was not my choice to make. The disease was stronger than I was; always, always stronger than I was.

But over time it wasn't. You can indeed make a choice, and my advice is to try it once, then again, and again, and again. It may not work the first time. It may not even work the 25th time, but you may see a glimmer of hope on the 26th, and that is the beginning, the moment you learn to cherish and build on. Every time you challenge the disease, it loses power and you gain power. You have to learn not to be discouraged by the first attempts because there will be many. I had to remind myself that it took years for my disease to fully develop, so recovery would not be a quick step either.

After reading *Seat of the Soul*, I realized that my eating disorder became a true addiction: an addiction to the scale, an addiction to exercise, an addiction to calorie calculation, an addiction to bulimia episodes, an addiction to self deprecation. I could not imagine life without doing these things. I would panic if I lost a measuring spoon, be agitated if I was unable to exercise. My personality became one of self centeredness, anger and resentment. If I couldn't get my fix, everyone knew it. These addictions are resistant to the energy of your soul and you must recognize this.

Perhaps the most useful aspect of the book was being reminded that wholeness means being true to yourself, with the courage to face your demons, your trouble, the truth. I equate the word wholeness to wellness. To me in order to be whole, to be well, you need to be honest (there is that word again). Honest with your illness, how you feel, how you feel about others and how you feel about yourself. It is looking at why you have an eating disorder. What purpose is it serving? And it does serve a purpose. The road to the rainbow is to better serve the purpose, to serve your needs in a healthy and productive manner.

Gary Zukav is one of many authors who have been of inspiration to me. Other books include: *Courage to Heal*, as well as a series of books by Sark and Louise Hay and a recent purchase, *Thoughts from the Seat of the Soul* by Gary Zukav, a handbook of meditations that I strongly recommend. These are helpful in terms of information and building the foundation of a positive attitude, which are crucial in wiping out the disease.

CHAPTER TWO IN REVIEW

One of the first things I was struck by when re-reading Chapter two was the issue of appreciating a relapse of any magnitude.

So important is the ability to attribute triggers to the relapse. Who were you with? What was the situation? What events lead to the situation? What time of day was it? Where were you? Were you rested or sleep deprived? And what about those details was really at the bottom of what was bothersome? Looking at every detail helps to understand the relapse and most importantly, assists you in learning from the relapse.

Ironically this tool, this "in tune awareness," has served as a wonderful life tool as I continue on my life's journey. What you quickly learn as a recovered individual is that life is life. It is wonderful, full of joy, surprises, happiness, kindness and love. But it also comes with sorrow, disappointment and loss. The Ying and Yang of life's balance. Recovering does not mean you are immune from pain but being well allows you to ride the wave of life's challenges.

I have been asked about the issue of life challenges and the ability to move past the urge to revert to old behaviours, especially during life's pressures and tragedies.

Since originally writing the book in 2003 life has happened as it will, with great joy and happiness but many challenges as well, unfortunately including painful loss and moments that cause you to question your life's purpose. While recovered and thankfully so, I share the honesty that there have been moments of self doubt and frustration so strong I thought I couldn't get past them, but guess what? By using the techniques I initially wrote about in the book, feeling to heal, letting it out through letters, journals and using my "voice," the moment(s) passed.

Two events were particularly challenging, with both happening within months of each other. In October of 2004 I went in for a routine surgery to remove polyps from my uterus. I had the same routine surgery a few years earlier and there was no cause to think this surgery would be any different.

The first operation was a simple day surgery in and out, back home and the next day back to my regular routine.

I went in for the second surgery around noon and expected to be out and in recovery around 1-1:30 pm. I woke up at 6 pm only to look down at my stomach covered in stitches and wet blood; I knew something had gone terribly wrong.

The doctor came to sit by my side to let me know there were complications during surgery. The surgical scope had ruptured the uterus causing extensive bleeding; specialists were called in due to the fear that further damage had been done to the bowel. Thankfully there was no damage to the bowel but damage was done to the uterus, and it was removed.

A very strange overwhelming emotion came over me after that news as I lay on the gurney, tears of loss. As a child, and adult for that matter, I never really had a desire to have children. Add to that years of abuse to my body due to a variety of eating disorders and lack of a period for over a decade, and it was suggested to me by most professionals to think long and hard about giving birth. I even had my tubes tied during the first polyps surgery but now something was final, a decision taken "out of my control," and I cried. Why? I didn't want to have children anyway. Why? Up until that moment it was an emotion I had never felt before.

A hospital stay was the result. A routine surgery changed my routine and became a life challenge for me, of which I did surpass. In what way you may ask? This experience was a huge reminder of my 1991 near death experience hospital stay. The physical discomfort of bloating and difficulty with bowel movements was too real. Well over ten years later the physical intensity from 1991 returned as if it had happened yesterday.

When I was able to return home my physical activities were greatly restricted for over six weeks, another challenge. My life at that point, and continuing today, is one of realistic balance, proper nutrition, regular sleep and moderate exercise. This "bump" in the road challenged that routine which in turn definitely challenged my psyche. Following is a journal entry describing this frustration…

Journal Entry
October 17th 2004
   Psychologically I think this recovery is different for someone who has recovered from an eating disorder. For me the balanced routine has been interrupted due to no regular exercise and difficulty with normal bowel movements. The bloating, and feeling like any food that goes in because I am not going to the bathroom, is literally going no where. Like the analogy I have used before about the car needing gas, it's like the gas is overflowing.

   It's not the physical recovery though that is hard it is fighting the mental challenge. I am finding it pretty tough.

What got me through was writing about the struggles and verbalizing the frustrations with family and friends; just to be heard was key. As well, I also told the physician and his assistants about my struggles and how this complication, while difficult for anyone, brings with it additional challenges in recovery for those with an eating disorder. There was a sense of empowerment to express this to the physician, to inform and educate him on the disease and how this mistake served as a challenge. It all goes back to expression, feeling to healing, a technique while not always easy, guaranteed to get you passed life's hurdles.

The second life event that sent a major shock to my system was the death of not only a past physician, but more importantly a dear friend, Dr. Doug Shrives, to whom this book's edition is dedicated. As we know, death is indeed a part of life and no matter what, that loss is painful. And while I have lost other wonderful members of my family since writing the first edition of this book, it was the suddenness of Doug's passing that was so difficult to comprehend.

I had just been up to visit Doug while attending a meeting at Sheena's Place in Toronto. I had actually stayed with him at his home. He entertained as he always did, top notch with a dining experience at Scaramouche, one of Toronto's top restaurants.

What I remember most about the visit was how happy he was. Doug had his own demons to battle while growing up but he had taken them head on and won. He had a partner he adored and life was good.

A couple of days later my aunt tracked me down. She asked if I was sitting down; "Why?" was my response. She said she had no other way of telling me but that Doug had died. He apparently suffered from a rare heart disease and while sudden, died peacefully. The news hit me like a lightening bolt; I truly didn't know what to do with the emotions inside.

Writing in my journal helped me to cope. Following is my journal entry…

Journal Entry
December 5th 2004
   Doug, you were so much more than a friend to me, I know I don't need to explain, always understood… a

given.

Tears are falling and my heart aches.

Last night I went running, well, more like walking our route in Kingston...a wonderful picture of you tucked on the inside of my vest...next to my heart.

It was cold, waves crashing, the strongest winds I've ever seen, ever felt.

I cried, I screamed wondering...Why?...Why you? Why now? Then, just like the waves, thoughts of you rushed over you, around you, beside you...then to me.

Thoughts and memories of...what you have given me, what you have taught me, the remarkable life lessons from a remarkable man.

You taught me about the power we all have within us, the strength of our right to choose, the right to set boundaries, the right to take care of ourselves for if we don't the idea that you can help others is merely a façade. For the truth is when you find that inner peace with your inner self...it all just works.

You had and will continue to have that peace.

You taught me that honesty doesn't need to hurt but that it is the strongest tool to growth. You taught me to laugh at personal obsessions instead of fighting them. The key is to embrace them, direct them in a positive direction; you helped me to understand that it indeed can be done.

You taught me to be a better person...no...that's not it. You taught me to be the best person I can be, not better than, just the whole of myself.

Doug, you added colour to my life, and you know how I love colour. You have added a very special hue to my life's rainbow. You have made it...

Kinder
Gentler
Richer
Deeper
Stronger
Brighter

For all that you have given me, taught me, my friend I say thank you Doug and I love you.

He was quite a man. I continue to hold Doug's spirit close and in my heart. In a way he is like my conscience, an inner guide. In my walkman case is a picture of Doug and I, hard to believe four years old now. While worn on the edges the smiles on our faces, the love and connection in our hearts are fully intact.

I share this story because I think it is important to relate a life tragedy while recovered and the fact that I survived it intact, and carried on. Instead of suppressing or avoiding the feelings I used my journal to express the pain and loss. I gave myself permission to feel in order to heal, a key concept to not only understand but to practice on your road to recovery, and frankly key to understanding life in general.

In the preceding text of Chapter Two I describe the importance of attitude and using quotes as a good motivator to the day. This is still crucial to how I live my life today. Following are some more wonderful quotes noted in journals since first writing the book. And yes, people continue to call to get motivated themselves, or at least think in a new direction. I hope you will enjoy these additions as well. To those wonderful individuals who coined these phrases I thank you in advance for your words of wisdom in that often no acknowledgment was given to the reference.

"You may not always get what you want, but you will get what you need."

"What ever the struggle continue the climb, it may be only one more step to the summit."
- Diane Westlake

"Where there is great doubt there is great awakening."

"It is in the very heart of our activity that we search for our goal."

"Slow down, and the thing you are chasing will come around and catch you."

"Live Simply, Love Generously, Care Deeply, Speak Kindly"

"Be kinder than necessary for everyone you meet is fighting some kind of battle."

"When you learn forgiveness, you will find love and when you find love-God's light will shine upon you."
- From the movie *Into the Wild*

"Love many, trust few, always paddle your own canoe"
- M.J. Sarginson

As well as quotes, there are sometimes short poems or sayings that seem to hit a nerve for me. Following is a poem written on a park bench close to where I live and it seems to speak volumes to me, and I hope for some of you as well. It is written in memory of a F. Joseph Chithalen 1967-1999 and reads as follows...

"A specific soul patiently awaits, on that particular park bench, for a specific soul, for them to be united again. While waiting here she gets transported. She can almost sense and perceive him and relive the moments. Not so much finding herself in the moments, but instead finding the moments in herself."

On a recent visit to the Canadian War Museum I was particularly struck by the following…

"History is not just the story you read. It is the one you write. It is the one you remember or denounce or relate to others. It is not predetermined. Every action, every decision, however small, is relevant to its course. History is filled with horror, and replete with hope. You shape the balance."

When I read the above it spoke to me in terms of our lives and our own histories and our role and responsibility in it. Through our choices we do indeed shape our lives. You, through your choice of being well, will indeed change the course of your life.

I cannot stress enough the importance of using these quotes, poems and sayings in their ability to support you through your stages of recovery and how they can be of support through your daily life. Find the ones that speak to you. Keep them handy, for they can sometimes be the words of positive redirection; I know they certainly have been so for me over the years.

Another portion of this chapter discussed the issue of honesty during recovery through all its stages. As we know, it begins by being honest about the disease and its hold on you, but more than that, honest about the real feelings that caused the nucleus of the disease in the first place.

Often during a presentation or in a one on one conversation I ask the sufferer, "What is really going on? Who are you mad at? What is making you sad, hurt, angry, lonely?" Personally, the disease buried my voice, clouded what was really going on, and I believe it does the same for all sufferers. The key is finding your voice and letting it out.

At a recent presentation I looked at the crowd of sufferers and family members and discussed this voice and the importance of uncovering and letting it out. I looked out at the room and said, "I am looking at you and cannot see a zipper on anyone's lips." We have the power to speak and describe what we are feeling. People sometimes think we need to put feelings in a certain package to make meaning of them. For me the beginning of the process was just to allow the feeling to be real, not necessarily understand it, but feel it. If I felt sad or angry I had to learn how to let it flow and be just as it is. Often it is this stage alone that is all that's necessary to move forward.

It is uncomfortable at first because the emotions can often be buried deep inside you. The eating disorder became the way to avoid them. However what you learn with every day you continue with the disease is that the disease only compounds the problem. What I have found is that once you learn to feel what it is you're feeling, you recognize that the intensity will dissipate once given the respect that is necessary.

But how do you deal with them, especially if intense and overwhelming? This is a question I have often been asked since first writing the book back in 2003. Again, I would be lying if I said that to deal with your feelings is an easy process, but once you find outlets that work for you, you'll actually wonder what took you so long, and doesn't that sound good?

When dealing with an intense emotional situation or feeling, go to a place on your own where you feel safe. For some it may be your home, maybe a car, a park, a field or by the water and just let it out. If it is a scream, scream, if it is cry, cry. If at home scream as loud as you can into your pillow, or take the pillow and hit the bed with it as hard as you can, but the key is to let it out in a safe manner.

If that option feels too daunting for you try writing out what you're feeling. A journal might be useful or as I have mentioned previously write a letter about what you're feeling. It can often be powerful, especially if you're struggling with feelings towards a certain individual. Write the letter, get it out, then burn it. It really does provide a healthy release and an outlet that you will have to try yourself to appreciate its value.

A sufferer who I recently worked with tried this method and it worked tremendously for her. She had issues concerning three early childhood friends who used to taunt her in Grade 3 and even though the situation was years in the past, the pain for her was relived daily. I asked her, if she felt like it, to write those girls a letter, and again if she felt comfortable to read it to me. Over a period of time she did in fact write the letter. During a subsequent meeting she brought it with her and I asked her to read it to me. She said she couldn't, her actual comment being, "Meredith I am so angry in this letter, I use such horrible language, I'd be embarrassed to read it to you, what you'll think of me." I told her it was safe. That I knew the anger was not directed at me. She read the letter, and yes she was angry, but she got it out. After reading the letter, we went outside with a lighter and an ashtray and burned the letter. We came in and sat for a moment, then I asked her how she felt…"Amazing!" was the response.

I asked her if she would mind writing about that experience for this edition. Following, in her own words, is what she felt after expressing these buried feelings she had kept inside for so long…

> *Keeping things in is like a cancer that can eat away at your very core. Even the tiniest issues can build up over time if they are not let go, festering away and consuming your waking moments. Holding in negative thoughts will affect every aspect of your life – your sleep, your relationships with others and your job because they become so huge and take up so much of your energy. To let out your feelings, your opinions, is to breathe. The cathartic experience of letting go of issues, or even just voicing them to another adds so much clarity to your life.*
>
> *There is no shame in saying "I need to get this off my chest." It can be one of the greatest gifts you can give to yourself. The sooner you get rid of the poison and the negativity and worry you have inside of you, the lesser the chance that it will become a cancer inside of you!*

You can discuss the letter with a therapist, a friend or family member who you feel safe with. The most important thing here is "getting out the struggle that is within."

Additional techniques that I use now that help me to deal in a positive way with every day (and sometimes more intense) challenges…

➢ Simply removing myself physically from the immediate environment is often helpful to quickly regroup. This can be as simple as moving from one room to another. Even better though is going outside, and just breathe in the air.

➤ 20-30 minutes of physical activity. Note this is not an excessive workout. Once fully recovered a full workout is possible but during recovery a simple short walk can help change one's perspective.

➤ Read - always have literature handy around you that is motivating and supports wellness. Three authors who I highly recommend, their book bindings are staring at me as I write this now, are Wayne Dyer, Eckhart Tolle and Melody Beattie. Even if you randomly open their books and read one paragraph, I can guarantee you that your thoughts will change.

➤ Water - I have found that if I can walk around or view water, be it a lake, river or stream, it serves as a very soothing, calming effect. Along with looking at water, being in it can also be of comfort. The buoyancy of the water, to freely float, also has a calming sensation. There is something about water and the vastness of it as I have mentioned before that can just seem to put issues in perspective. If you don't live near water or have access to a pool, you can always soak in a warm tub or feel the droplets from a shower…no excuse…give it a shot!

➤ Heat/Sunshine - another thing I do that I find wonderful to regroup, especially during the cold winter months, is to either go to a sauna or a quick visit to a tanning booth (I know dermatologists will not agree with that one). In the sauna I often take a copy of a book written by one of the previously mentioned authors to warm up not only my body but my soul. I often talk aloud in there to God or the higher power about the issue at hand, asking for guidance to help resolve the issue.

➢ Music/Art - even if you don't consider yourself artistic I encourage you to explore creative outlets. Painting, drawing, model making or knitting, the options are endless and can serve as a wonderful outlet not only for creativity but personal expression. Through the colours you pick and the medium you use, you are in control of the end result in a healthy way. The key is to be free, no judgment, just let it all out. The same can be done through music. Try your hat at learning an instrument; for me it has been the guitar. Equally effective is simply listening to music. Broaden your horizons with your musical tastes and explore your emotions through the variety of musical genres we are so fortunate to enjoy today.

➢ Play a game - recently I watched a news program that had a segment on a young woman who had battled and won her struggle with an eating disorder. Interestingly she and her mother noted that playing scrabble helped her on her road to recovery. Something about changing focus allowed her time with her mother without the screaming, and for a moment to cease focusing on the obsession. Playing the game helped, step by step, to more moments without the obsessions. I share this because I think it is a great idea. As I have always said, how incredibly helpful would it be if all of us who have recovered shared these tips with those who are struggling.

These are but a few of the actual hands on tangible tips to help you deal with those internal moments of conflict.

In Chapter Two I ended by discussing attitude and primarily discussed how the book *Seat of the Soul* by Gary Zukav was very helpful for me in understanding myself and my soul. Over the past five years I have done much work on that area of my life which has provided me with continued health and stability.

I continue to read literature or expose myself to positive messages that only reinforce what I wrote about in the first edition. In this chapter I write, "If you radiate illness, pessimism, sadness, fear and suspicion then that is indeed what you receive in return." Ironically this same message is the core focus of the book *The Secret*. The core message in that book is the "Law of Attraction," which is what I talked about in my book as well, just at the time I was not aware of the phrase. If we all just realized that if we are in a negative situation be it health, finances or relationships, we are probably sending out energy that is attracting it. I would encourage all to pick up this book if you have not already done so. This is a book with a powerful, simple message that if you're ready to embrace it, could indeed change your life.

CHAPTER THREE

Treatment: Traditional and Non-Traditional
Don't Be Afraid to Think Outside the Box

Treatment is such an important area of recovery. I am an advocate now, but it did not start out that way. I fought it every step of the way. Is this an easy part of the recovery process? No. At least it wasn't for me.

First there is the stigma attached to treatment, especially when it involves psychiatric treatment. "She must be crazy!" That is what I thought others would think of me once they learned I was seeing a "shrink" or was in a "One Who Flew Over the Cuckoo's Nest" rehab facility. Health and recovery have proven to me that to seek treatment is a sign of health and strength, not a sign of weakness or illness. It is when you don't seek help that recovery becomes impossible. While I firmly believe that recovery starts with you, it cannot be done alone.

I can't remember every doctor I have seen, techniques attempted or facilities visited but I do know that collectively they all served some benefit or purpose. Would I say that one in particular stood out in terms of effectiveness? Yes, my one-on-one therapy.

Today, I no longer see my therapist on a regular basis.

How it was that day when she looked at me and said, "Our work is done and the rest is up to you." She wasn't deserting me, but instead had given me the tools to continue my recovery independently. This process took over ten years. There is no quick fix.

My therapist, while having every right to give up on me,

didn't. But she didn't because we were the right fit. You may go through several therapists or counsellors before you find the right one for you, but it is worth making the effort.

In one journal entry after my therapist asked me to think about the work she and I had done together, just prior to that work being completed, I wrote the following:

Journal Entry
February 27th 1997

Having to look at me and the truth has stirred up much. Perhaps most overwhelming is that I no longer worry about the future but rather today. The here, the now. It's what I have avoided for years.

Going in circles it's the pattern, there isn't a wall at all; if there is it's in my mind. And about the circle, imaginary too, created by no one else but myself. How embarrassing to have to admit but it is an essential step. This really isn't anything new but having to re-evaluate my therapy has made me have to face it.

When I started therapy, it was an "out" to satisfy everyone else, to get them off my back and to make everyone feel better that I was seeking help. So it started. It was years of performing, being physically present, mentally absent then thankful to leave the seat.

Then a subtle change. Being exposed to a listener, a mirror to myself, was doing something, nothing earth-shattering but change and a glimmer of hope. Maybe I could be fixed. Everyone around me was and is looking for a quick fix and so did I until recently. I haven't been fixed but what therapy has done is give me the tools, the equipment to be my own superintendent. The choice I need to make is to use them. Is there more that can be done now in a session once or twice a week? No.

What am I feeling?

That it's on to the next lesson, the next test. Bridget, my therapist, has given me the tools, the reading, the techniques to cope with what I view as my problems or personality quirks. Like a bike with training wheels, it's time they came off. As Louise Hay says, "It really is only us, and either we use the power we have wisely or we misuse the power."

What I would like to say to Bridget is thank you. I know I have not been easy, as she has often said, frustrating, but she hung in there, believed and worked with me, knowing what tools and information would be applicable to me and for that I will be forever grateful. While it may have left her questioning our work, please know it has worked. I now just need to use what she has given me. I have a better knowledge in order to change and be well. I just need to wake up and realize I have the knowledge, and I have the power.

What were some of the tools? What was it about therapy that helped? To have an objective listener is the first plus. A therapist should have no vested interest in your life personally, and if at all possible, no connection to your life either. I feel this element of therapy is critical.

It is the aspect of being able to explore what you are feeling no matter how bizarre, hurtful, shameful or uncomfortable you may be about discussing them. You need to get it out in a safe, monitored environment, and with a good therapist this is what happens. Once you know what the feelings are, you become better able to deal with them in the real world. Role playing helps, and being able to be real is the best feeling in the world. With my therapist, I was able to explore my past and recognize the damage that had been done. But more importantly I realized those painful things were in the past, no longer happening to me now. Recognizing that pain, talking about them, putting them in present context, allowed me to let them go and move on.

For some of us reaching that level of honesty takes longer than for others, but when it happens recovery seems to speed up and make more sense...almost as if the blinders have been taken off.

What is often difficult, particularly for people in rural areas, is access to a professional. It's even more difficult accessing a specialist in the area of eating disorders. The crucial thing is getting help. Maybe it begins with your family doctor or GP, school, health unit or church. You need to talk to somebody. Begin somewhere. Remember, it is the beginning. In my case, access to a specialist was a challenge. It started with a GP, then a friend who was a psychiatrist who referred me to another, Bridget, who in turn would suggest reading material and other information. It is a process, a continual road, this road to the rainbow.

What were some of the areas we worked on or techniques / tools learned in therapy?

(A) Exploration of Relationships

One of the important things achieved in therapy was discussion of the past, and the relationships with the people in my life. I needed to work through what they were and what they represented in my life, positive or negative. I am happy to say that because of my regained wellness, health prevails within the relationships of my support system, but it certainly was not always that way. Over the years some of my relationships have strengthened while others were severed.

Therapy has helped me understand the role that each relationship has played in my life.

A review of my journals reminded me of the terrible impact my illness had on me and those around me.

Every day I had my own inner battle and it transferred into battles with family and friends. I resented comments. I did not like intervention and felt as though there was a conspiracy going on. There were conversations discussing me, but never including me. I felt paranoid and angry towards everyone. Why couldn't they leave me alone? Why did they not try to understand? I felt like the solution of putting me in hospitals was their way of getting rid of me.

Understanding their own pain and struggle with my disease did not begin until I admitted I had a problem, but in some cases that realization and understanding of their pain came too late.

I could not see the interest of others in me as caring or concern, but rather, as invasion of privacy. I resented that concern. It angered me.

I remember receiving a letter from my Uncle Dave who had divorced my father's sister years earlier. I was in a clinic in Florida and was stunned to receive this letter of concern. Following are some excerpts from the letter:

June 29, 1991

Dear Meredith,

    First let me apologize for sending you a personal typed letter. I've always been told that personal letters must be handwritten, and that typing is only for business letters. However, to be truthful, I can type far faster than I can write, and my handwriting is largely unreadable, even for me. So anyway, I'm typing the letter.

By this time I hope that you are starting to feel a bit better. I understand that you are not allowed any phone calls home or anywhere else for some time. However, letters are OK. I hope that includes letters in to the clinic too.

When I started thinking about writing to you it occurred to me that I don't think I have ever written to you at any time. When you were younger I think I may have put messages on birthday cards but that was all. Like Davy, Dorcas and Hunter you were just there; part of the world of Brockville and our family. A lot of water has gone under the bridge since those days. I've been away from Brockville and returned. You've grown up and married, travelled a good bit too, and because of circumstances we've kind of lost touch with each other. The world is often like that, but family is always family, and it is at times like these that we all wake up and realize how important each of us is to all the rest. I want you to know that I care very much about you, and wish very much for your success in overcoming a very difficult and demanding problem. I have been and will continue to be thinking about you in the weeks to come. I know your parents will keep me up to date on any developments, and I'll very much look forward to them being positive ones.

That may sound like too much sloppy sentimentality from an uncle that you don't even see very often, but it is meant very sincerely.

Bobbie just called to say that dinner is ready so I must close. She sends her love too, and said to say she admires your courage. Stick to it, we know you can do it. I echo her sentiments. We'll look forward to seeing you back at the tennis club soon, and on the mend.

> *All our best,*
> *Much love Uncle Dave*

I was stunned by this letter initially. I did not see it as concern at all but rather as "this is none of your business." I am so thankful I kept the letter to now appreciate it for the wonderful loving concern it expressed. It is sad for me to look back on this letter now. Both Uncle Dave and his wife have since passed away. I never got a chance to thank him for the letter but I have to believe he somehow knows. My health today is proof of that.

One thing has become very clear to me in terms of relationships: it is impossible to give to relationships in your life when you are not well. The falseness of the commitment is not fair to the other person or to yourself. I hated myself, wanted to die and really did not believe that my life would be a long one. I thought bringing in others would solve my problems, make it all better. It didn't. If anything, in some ways doing so made things worse because I then was burdened by guilt. This person was too good for me; I felt unworthy, old messages continued to resurface. I realize now it is not that I was unworthy, but rather, I was unhealthy, which can sabotage any relationship. For some, the relationship was severed forever. For others, it has been an extremely painful and lengthy journey back.

Through therapy, I learned about myself and my connections with people. I was using the eating disorders as a way to cope with all that I couldn't handle in my life. Instead of dealing with my emotional issues and concerns, I controlled them by controlling my weight. As I have noted before, I have dealt with those relationships that are no longer a part of my daily life but am thankful to have had them be a part of my life. Without one in particular I think I would be dead. If I never marry again, I have been blessed. Bill tried so hard to help me, was so committed and I couldn't give it back. If there is one person I wish I could have spared the pain, it is Bill. He tried everything. He was an angel; he was my angel and I will be forever thankful to have had him in my life.

Bill and I divorced some time ago, both of us realizing it was the right thing to do. He is now happily re-married and I am happy for him. I realize that some people come into your life for a reason, a season or a lifetime, and I have learned to appreciate this. What is important is appreciating the gift of that special time. I know that I probably would not be alive without Bill, but it was not meant to be forever, and I know that now. The termination of that relationship was the most painful decision I have ever made, but I believe for both of us, it was the right one. I had to start the next part of my journey alone. I believe we loved each other enough to know that the best thing to do was to let each other go.

I think about Bill every day, and what fills my heart is knowing I did not (although it came painfully close) kill his spirit. I'm content that he has been able to live and love and be happy. He gave me love, support, understanding and wings.

I also learned through therapy that it is detrimental to recovery to be in an unhealthy relationship or one that has run its course. I have also experienced this type of relationship. While aspects of the relationship were good, I felt unable to say how I was really feeling, and even though I was on the road to recovery, I felt out of control. I began reverting to behaviour that was comforting and familiar, whether it was food restriction, exercise or a binge and purge period.

I have spoken to many women who did not feel

comfortable expressing their feelings to their partners. I have also talked to women whose partners consistently criticized their appearance and weight, commented on their food intake, and pointed out their lack of exercise. If you have self confidence, you probably don't allow these comments to go unchallenged in the first place, but this is not the case if you are suffering from an eating disorder and haunted by low self esteem.

Seek counselling. Convince your spouse or partner to participate. You can't recover if the relationship is a problem. The problems do not have to deal directly with eating disorder issues. Perhaps it is an abusive relationship, stifling, or controlled. The key is to deal with it or get out. Often we think our life is made complete by being in a relationship, but in reality, it is better to have nobody than the wrong body.

Is the relationship healthy? Do you feel good about it? Does the relationship add value to your life? Does it make you a better person? Would life be empty without that person? If you answer "No" to these questions, it's time to get out.

Getting out of a negative relationship can be difficult and painful, but in the long run it is better for everyone involved, even though it may not seem so at the time. For me, it has not been easy. I don't like to hurt anyone but sometimes it needs to happen in order for you to move on. There is pain in the process, but clarity in the end.

In order to get well, you need to be surrounded by positive energy. After severing a negative relationship, I felt a freedom and an independence that is hard to explain. Taking control of a bad situation became empowering.

Your positive support system should expand to embrace many: family, a friend, a teacher, a co-worker, a religious leader or a support group.

The key is a positive environment. I had to make painful

decisions to sever ties with negative relationships because they were degrading, not nurturing. Do I resent the loss of those relationships? No. I am thankful for the good times and keep those memories, but I now concentrate on the positive, not the negative.

For me the most important support system has been family. I thank God every day for mine.

Has this been an easy road for those in my life? Absolutely not! There have been words. There have been tears. There have been yelling matches. But with time, the result has been health and love.

Most telling were the effects of anorexia on my family. This disease was damaging not only me, but them. It was difficult for my parents on a number of fronts. Initially, it was lack of information and resources. In a small city, access to either was limited, but today the internet and increased awareness of eating disorders have helped immensely.

They also had to struggle with their inability to fix the problem. Not only was I out of control with this illness, but to a degree, so were they. I can only imagine the agony of watching their child fading away before their eyes, and not knowing what to do to stop it.

My mother recently reminded me of the hospital stay that nearly became my last. I was in the emergency department in The Brockville General and a nurse who Mom knew asked her if she was bringing in her mother. That's how old I looked at 80 pounds. I was then in a room, curled up in a fetal position when my muscles cramped because of potassium deficiency. I remember the pain. I said, "Mom I am going to die." She put her mouth next to mine, breathing air, breathing life into me, and said, "You are not going anywhere." She was not going to let me die. She knew I was not meant to die. She told me how angry she was. So angry at me, at this disease. I realized I wasn't the only one struggling. So was every one else.

My mother and I struggled. As we both are headstrong and stubborn, it was at times a volatile situation. Once when doing a class presentation on eating disorders with my mother in attendance, she was asked by one of the students if she ever hated me. My mom's response: "At times, I hated her guts, hated not so much Meredith but the disease and what the disease was doing to my daughter and our family." While it was painful to hear those words, I was touched by her overwhelming honesty. This disease was hurtful and made us all angry, but we had to be able to say how we felt.

This element of honesty is important for the family. Everyone needs to feel, speak and be heard. As a family, we had to let others in and appreciate that this would be a long process. Mom's patience with me often ran short because of her need to fix me, and the subsequent frustration with her inability to do so. She has often said that the beginning of my road to the rainbow started with my own commitment to wellness. Her energy was better spent supporting the message of commitment to recovery once I recognized it. She believed in me all along; knew I had the strength, knew I had the power. Her biggest gift has been her belief in me, and since that Boxing Day in 1991 when she breathed her strength into me, that belief has grown stronger.

With Dad, the process has been very different. We have come a long way to a wonderful friendship. Today there is a love and respect for one another. This part of my long journey has been worth the wait.

As with Mom, Dad struggled to understand the disease. I think he probably understood it better than anyone but that did not make dealing with me any easier.

Following is a letter my dad wrote to me sixteen years ago. I include it because I feel it sheds a lot on my disease and its effect on me and my family. It is a very special letter, painful at the time, but words I now consider a gift.

The following letter was written on the 14th of July 1992, given to me on July 24th:

Dear Meredith:

I'm writing this letter after an evening conversation with your Mum, and after sitting up in the morning hours thinking about you and your life.

Knowing where to begin is not difficult. I wish to start by saying: "I love you. Very Much." And it is this deep affection that drives me to put on paper those things we may not have discussed yet, or felt awkward about expressing, though I'm sure some of the things you will read here are not new.

The other reason I have chosen this method of communication stems from Betty's comment that, right now, there seems to be a sense of tension when we are together. You feel under examination. I find watching you emaciate before my eyes more painful each time I look.

But avoidance will not solve anything. That is simply an out-of-sight-but-not-out-of-mind situation. So, please accept these observations, these explanations, and these suggestions as a collection of things I wanted to say. And please believe me, they come from the heart.

In your case, there have been three stages, though they seem to have been in decades, not quarter centuries, and I agonize over how you can break out of the path you are on, so your life can follow a more normal phasing; so you can participate in life with zest and energy and fun; so you can be healthy enough to have a body functioning as a woman's body should; even, so you might have children, and watch them grow and develop too. If life is judged by its quality, then I would love to see you well enough to enjoy the quality you deserve. Suffering you've done enough of.

To me, Mer, your first stage, those first ten years, saw growth follow in the normal pattern. You were my floppy-socked, loving daughter. You were a delight. There was not an ounce of meanness in you, and the ability to attract and hold friends, something precious you certainly retain today, was part of your uniqueness, part of what set you that notch above so many others.

The next phase, from ten to twenty, contained the hurt.

With that second decade we saw the anorexic behaviour begin, and, as is so often the case, we did not really understand what was happening until the behaviour was established. I must admit, reading the many journals on eating disorders, we as parents share with other anorexic's Moms and Dads many characteristics as well: strong willed, achievers, goal oriented, and in my case, successful in following a doctor's plan to lose weight. I remember, on several occasions, giving both you and Kingsley hell, from my lofty pinnacle, about the evils of too much animal fat, refined sugar and junk food. Just what a couple of growing kids wanted to hear, right?

The problem worsened for you, though Mer, in the third decade, between twenty and thirty, when the disease became chronic.

From my perspective, however, as the realist you know me to be, I must look at the results of this last half decade, and without doubt, you are more emaciated today than you were five years ago. What will happen, if this continues, in the next half decade, or more immediately, between now and the time you would be thirty?

Mer, I have read the statistics. So have you. Between 14 and 21 percent of anorexic patients die. I can't let this happen to you! You must not let this happen to you! My fear, though, is that the days are passing; you are not getting "better", which I guess means you continue to lose weight or at best do not gain any, and at some point your poor, poor body is going to say: "Enough."

If I track how we have attacked this horrible disease and how you have responded, therein also can be found a pattern. Looked at as a graph, it would appear as a line slowly dropping, with brief reverses upward. These positive changes would result from intervention on our part, or on Bill and our parts, and they included hospitalization or bed rest or threats about what would happen if you didn't "improve". In each case, there was some progress, but shortly thereafter the slide would start again, and more weight would be lost.

I think your biggest improvement came after your worst low, on Boxing Day. I know you remember it well. We almost lost you. It was frightening for us, but even more frightening for you to know your body was shutting down because of starvation and badly imbalanced blood. Watching the results of that intravenous drip, however, as it slowly restored your body's fluids and chemical balance, was like watching a miracle. The speed with which you bounced back when

Ensure was added was astounding. The weight gain, difficult for you to accept, took years off your appearance, and I began to hope, for the first time in years, that the graph had taken a positive turn that would not be reversed. I was wrong.

Initially, you were faithful to your Doctor and his regular blood work and checkups. Then, as the weight began to drop, you interrupted the regularity of those visits. Once again, the graph took a downturn.

Most recently, I have told you something must be done. Soon. And I suggested that if nothing happened in the way of improvement by the time I returned from up north, we would have to act on your behalf.

Your response was fairly typical of what has happened over the years: set a plateau of achievement, and if met, the "punishment" (how you would perceive being put in hospital against your will) would be removed. Again, at first there were phone calls about incremental weight gain. At first. Then they stopped. Because behaviour hadn't changed. Through all this, Mer, we are trying to understand. But it's not easy.

Bets and I are aware just how ingrained the bulimia has become. You are expert at getting rid of nourishment without bothering others. But the result of that activity, your getting sicker and sicker, bothers me immensely.

Mer, when I travel, especially in airports, I often sit and watch the travellers go by. One yardstick I use constantly is this: can I see anyone who is as thin as my daughter? If "yes", how often does this happen? The answer, and I'm being frank and honest, is that I have only once seen someone whose body had atrophied to such an extent. She was in a wheel chair. Her age was indeterminate.

See what I mean? Prisoners of war, shown being released from various German camps in the last stages of WWII were often not as thin as you have become, and they certainly would have looked differently, if nourishment was available.

I mention these two things because I believe time is short. Your heart cannot take much more. You have lost considerable bone mass. Other organs have also been damaged, without doubt. Please forgive me for the bluntness, but it's what I believe, and I can't stand to watch you wither away any longer.

There are times when we too ask: "Why?" Is your behaviour, to some degree, continued as a form of punishment towards others as well as yourself? Is it to get your father's attention? Only you know the answer to these things, and even then, as the disease further dominates your mind, I wonder if the reasons matter any more.

Mer, Betty has often relayed that you seek recognition from me concerning a myriad of endeavours in which you may be involved, and when it comes to writing or speech making, you would like to move me to tears. There is a way to accomplish this. It would make me the happiest man, the happiest father, the happiest father-in-law. And that "way" is at your disposal: I would cry tears of joy to see you exhibit the kind of strength it would take to finally grapple this damn disease to the ground, and emerge the victor. And I know, and you know it can't be done alone. You need a concentrated, team effort. With that approach, I believe you have a chance. It can be done. Just say the word.

So, while I'm away for the next week, please think about your future. Think about your quality of life. Think about being well. And be realistic about getting there. From my side, I'll do whatever you wish if it gets you on the path to a healthy Meredith.

Now, let me close this letter the way it began, by saying I love you.

Remember, for every lock there is a key; for each action there is a reaction; for our problems there are solutions. What must be evident, however, is the will to change, to react, to solve, to unlock. That's where you come in, and, while embracing whatever help is required, you find the keys.

Love and affection,
Your Dad.

I now know when I read this letter that my father was dead right. Right about the pattern, right about what I needed to do. But back then I actually resented the letter because I was still so sick. I felt, "See, he never thinks I will be well. I am a failure." The perception you have, I had, was warped. The letter opened communication, even though not face to face. Dad's ability to say how he felt meant that doing so was okay. I needed to feel that within my family. The letter also contained other issues concerning the abuse and it opened the door to discussing those as well. This letter has served as an important element of my recovery, though Dad might not know how important it was. It became tangible evidence of honesty and feelings, and that it was okay to express them.

I also started to deal with issues concerning my father. We were able to discuss them. What I learned through this experience is that those closest to you are not mind readers. To assume they know how you feel, or you them, is a dangerous mistake. The truth, the reality can only be understood when shared. The truth indeed can set you free.

I feel fortunate in that I have parents who are extremely positive people. I think I challenged that, but they managed to hang on. How? I guess you would have to ask them, but they did all they could for me. Besides being supportive, they educated themselves on eating disorders (once they knew what was wrong) and still managed to maintain their own lives. I think that has been extremely important. Because they maintained their own life they were better equipped and stronger in order to deal with me!

They had to keep up their own lives because they needed a reprieve from me and my illness. Their strength kept me afloat. And though parents may not be your immediate support system, (often they can't be) whoever is a part of that support group, it is important that honesty, strength and optimistic support is ensured.

Within my family, communication became key. The old messages that rang in my head had transferred to my family. Earlier, I was afraid to voice my opinions and true feelings. Once I began this process, I realized it was not nearly as frightening as I'd imagined. It was, in fact, calming.

Having said all this about open communication and truth, I would hate you to think that every time you face your true feelings, what you really need, what you really want or don't want, that it will be easy. But keeping it all in is dangerous. Blocking out true thoughts and needs is where the disease continues to fester. When you release those hidden thoughts, the disease loses power.

It is important to think through how you will discuss these issues. This is where therapy and journaling come in handy. To run through what it is you are going to say will help you keep focused on what is really going on. I kept feelings and thoughts inside. Therapy and journaling helped to release those feelings and prepare me for the reality of expressing them.

Communication is important with both family and friends. In some situations, I had to explain to friends how certain comments became triggers or agitators. This was not an easy process, but my real friends understood and realized the importance to me of expressing these thoughts and feelings. For instance, I would say: "Could we please not talk about food, weight, exercise, being hungry or full, especially when out for lunch or supper together?" Many did not realize they were doing it. This took some practice, but it eventually worked.

Having these exchanges helped me to realize that those around me were not mind readers. Nor could they be walking on eggshells wondering whether something they did or said would send me in a downward spiral.

This is why cross information and education are so important. They are the best defences against this disease. You and those in your support system need to be as informed, as honest and as real as possible.

(B) Breathing

One of the things I learned in therapy was the importance of breathing. Sounds like a simple, obvious thing but I realized my breathing pattern affected me physically. My breathing seemed to stop at my chest. I didn't breathe all the way through. We practiced breathing during therapy, trying to breathe all the way through my body. It forced me to be in touch with my stomach, something I wanted to avoid. It was, and is, not separate from who I am. There was also something important about that full flow of oxygen that I can't explain, but I recommend that you try.

I also tried yoga to aid with my breathing, although for me this was not successful. However, I have met a number of people who swear by it, so give it a shot. It helped me to be more aware of my breathing, but I am afraid that with my type A personality, remaining calm was difficult. Yoga is wonderful for stretching your body and attempting to bring peace to your mind and body.

(C) Documentation

There was a procedure that Bridget used with me in therapy that was particularly helpful. This was in a chart format and helped me to deal with feelings in certain settings. I would create the following graph in my journal and it would help to see how my feelings would be influenced according to the time of day, and also whether I was alone or in the company of others.

	DAY	NIGHT
alone	feelings	feelings
with people	feelings	feelings

Throughout my journals I could see a definite pattern. The worst times were when I was alone and in the evening. Keeping track of these feelings became an important identification in recovery. After documenting this over a long period of time, the pattern became more and more evident. I had to see if there was indeed a pattern for me; I had to see something tangible. This tool allowed me to not only identify the patterns but also to interrupt them. I could stop those "bad times" by keeping busy with a to-do list, trying crafts, visiting a friend, writing a letter or calling someone.

I have often been asked what was on my to-do list? I always tried to have a list of healthy options handy to keep me busy and my mind off of weight, exercising, how to avoid food, or binging and purging. On the list were the usual: laundry, making the bed, doing dishes, etc. Also included were jobs that I had put off for one reason or another such as:

- ➢ organize the kitchen junk drawer, or any drawer for that matter
- ➢ put away loose photos in an album
- ➢ organize closets, jewellery, scarves and accessories
- ➢ clean the top shelves in the kitchen or over hutches
- ➢ dust everything on the shelf
- ➢ write a letter, e-mail or call an old friend

Also on the to-do lists were projects of some sort. Seeing results, positive results, was very important to me. Crafts became a significant part of my recovery journey. I would find one and away I'd go. For years it was crocheted afghans and then it was quilting. Almost everyone I knew received one of my "therapeutic comforts." It became a running joke. One afghan after another. Thank God for Wal-Mart's wool section. There was something comforting about being busy and creative and for the focus to be on a gift for someone else, not my weight. The aspect of doing something for someone else even if only momentary, took away the self centeredness.

I can't stress enough the importance of this list, whether you have it in your journal, on the fridge, in the bathroom or beside your bed. If the list serves as a deterrent even for a minute, it's worth it and you continue to build on it. Remember, minutes turn into hours, hours into days, and days into weeks.

Therapy also taught me that there are other ways to deal with stressful situations. From the chart, I realized which were stressful situations and learned to not only be aware of them but, with practice, learn to avoid them. I had a habit of jumping in with both feet into a situation that I knew would have grave results.

An example of this was buffet meals. Journal entries became proof that buffets (while I was trying to recover) were a dangerous temptation. Not only were buffets laden with food, but there was guilt everywhere. A part of me wanted it, wanted it all, and the other part of me said to avoid it. So I'd go, eat, and say, "If I am going to eat, I might as well have it all." This process set me up nicely for a binge and purge cycle for the remainder of the day. The guilt was overwhelming. My journals haven't lied. Every time I went to a buffet, I had the same problem. I then learned to pass on that offer. Do I go to them now? Yes, but did not for a few years. It wasn't worth it. Over time you realize what you are and aren't ready for. Journaling and keeping track of situations helped me to recognize triggers, and in turn to avoid them.

Another aid in stressful situations was squeezing something. Those stress balls are very handy. If not a stress ball, try a tennis ball, a towel, a toothpaste tube, etc. Just keep it underneath the table and clinch as needed. It is a much better option than fidgeting. But there is more to this. When I was ill, and attempting to get a grip on this illness, I was also trying to be aware of my overreaction to situations. I seemed to be a bundle of nerves and continually on edge. A simple comment would result in tears, or an angry outburst. The stress ball was an alternative to this. The harder I squeezed, the better I felt. Then I would go to my journal and write out the situation or comment, what it was that caused the problem, and how I was feeling about all of that. The next stage was discussing it in therapy so it came full circle in terms of understanding: a healthy pattern.

(D) Medication

Prozac is a drug that has often been prescribed for eating disorder sufferers. In the early 1990's, because of my low body weight, I was given Prozac in liquid form by drops. I couldn't handle it. I felt my equilibrium was off. I suffered from a severe case of dry mouth and it did not work for me. Almost ten years later, I am now on Prozac and it works wonders. People ask me: "What do you think it does for you?" I used to suffer anxiety, particularly around food; that was overwhelming, like a panic. What Prozac does for me is take that feeling away. I consider that I have a chemical imbalance of sorts and Prozac puts my chemistry back in sync.

I know many people say they would be ashamed to tell people they are on this antidepressant. Why? You would not tell a diabetic to stop taking insulin or an asthmatic to stop taking her medication. Their bodies lack something and these medications compensate for what's lacking, just as I believe Prozac does for me.

Is Prozac for everyone? No! At one time, it was not

appropriate for me. It was when my body weight was at a normal level that it seemed to be more of a benefit. As I have said before, this is my story and what has worked for me. Medication is definitely an option but is something you must discuss with your doctor. Keeping in mind each of us is different, medication may or may not be for you. The important thing is to explore the options.

(E) Hospitals and Long-term Treatment Facilities

Clinics are another traditional option. For some it involves a hospital stay, often long-term, especially when medical aid is required. For some this inpatient process works; for others it does not. I found hospital stays frightening, especially in my home town where I felt no one understood me. It's a given that the medical population can't know everything about every medical problem, but someone with an eating disorder requires a particular element of sensitivity.

I remember being in the hospital waking up feeling bloated beyond belief with an intravenous and a food tube attached to my body. My body didn't feel like mine. A nurse came in with a weigh scale and asked me to get on and weigh myself while she left the room. I freaked out! Remember, I was the girl weighing herself over fifty times a day with the most recent number being 78lbs only to wake up the next day weighing 96lbs! Anyone in her right mind would feel uncomfortable with an additional 18lbs added in one day, whether it was needed or not. I cannot describe the hysteria I went through that morning. I made sure everyone knew about it too. (Model patient I wasn't.) Then, to add insult to injury, another nurse came in asking how I was doing and that it was important that I "fattened up." Ugh!

I now appreciate the importance of education about eating disorders for medical professionals. While specialists are well informed on the facts, it is usually your GP or a health nurse who are the first to confront your illness. I am an advocate of educating this crucial population. It can do nothing but encourage recovery.

How did I feel about hospital stays? I hated them! They were not my choice but medically necessary. Do I see merit in them now? Yes, because without them I would probably be dead. There is a stage in an eating disorder that requires medical attention. I have come to realize that a hospital stay is required to provide emergency nutrition that you deprived yourself of for years. You don't like it but sometimes it has to be done. I remember the food tubes, getting up out of bed and emptying them in the sink, filling them with water, keeping the machine off until the nurses came back to check on me (I timed their visits). They would always wonder why thc darned things continued to clog. I would also go and exercise in a wing of the hospital that was closed and under renovations, intravenous and food bag in hand. The reality of it was that they had been able to restore my nutrition levels. I needed to have this happen despite hating every minute of it. Again, another important step on the road to the rainbow.

In fact eating disorder facilities are rare, often with a minimal number of beds available and frequently in a psychiatric ward. I recall waiting three hours to be admitted into one hospital, only to find my bed in a psych ward. I commented to my family, "If you leave me here, you really hate me." My mother's response, "I wouldn't leave a dead dog in here." We did not even take off our coats and told the doctor we were checking out. We all felt so desperate. I wanted to start getting better but there seemed to be limited options. I think this is when I began to realize the importance of taking advantage of any information, technique, therapy or other alternative options available.

I also attended a traditional rehab clinic in Florida called "The Willough." In terms of my attitude at the time, I wanted to try to get better, but still was not at a commitment level. I wasn't ready or honest. At that time, in the early 1990's, the clinic had two wings: one wing for eating disorder sufferers, primarily overeating and bulimia; the other for individuals having difficulty with drugs and drinking.

The Willough was set up more like a home than a hospital. Your day was completely filled with one-on-one therapy, group sessions, educational workshops, plus regular AA meetings. This facility believed in the importance of the 12 steps. They applied those 12 steps to overeating and for many this approach seems to work. In this program the group sessions were often heated. Today I would equate it to a Dr. Phil session, and there were some merits to this process as well.

Because of the double wing, I also learned a lot about problems regarding drugs and alcohol. I remember lying out in the sun (I was not allowed to go out walking at first) with a young man sentenced to rehab because of a crack cocaine problem and another woman there drying out from alcohol. I looked up at the sky and said, "What the hell am I doing here; this is pathetic," but soon realized there was someone else sitting there with a problem: me.

I met some wonderful people at The Willough, including my roommate, Alma. She was an older woman who had a very painful life and continued to suffer from a variety of eating disorders as her way of coping. I wonder about her often. If she reads this, I am hoping for the best for you my friend, always.

There were others. One I remember in particular, a woman named Linda, who when I first met her seemed very angry. She was an overeater and used food as a comfort. She had many other issues but anger exuded from her.

This woman was in my "group" which met several times a week. We looked at a variety of issues and often one person in particular was the focus of the session. Linda was in her last week of the month-long program and had been encouraged during this time to write a letter about what concerned or bothered her. On her last day she read the letter to the group; she was so angry. But something unusual happened to her after she had read the letter. A calmness came over her. A difference could be seen in her face, as if all the anger, hatred and pain had been lifted away.

After a person had gone through the month-long program, (this was a process I experienced over ten years ago) if she wrote and read a letter, she was then told to burn the letter in a big bin outside. She was also requested to ask someone to come along with her to do so. Linda asked me to come along with her.

While her letter burned, she told me how she had held on to the pain and anger, afraid of the consequences if she were to let it go. She now felt a difference inside. She had no false hopes that her work was over, but she felt she was now in a position to start without the emotional burden she had held inside. She hoped that one day I would be able to let go of what pained me, to let go of the fear and to let go of the obsessions. While I avoided the letter process until later on in my recovery, I thank Linda for her advice.

It seems throughout my recovery, the lessons may have been delayed but always learned.

In my recovery, it was as though all the things I tried initially appeared independently as failures. For example, I checked myself out of The Willough before my stay was complete. This was not a failure for the facility, but for me. I no longer look at the process that way. I look at it as not ready, not committed. I still had a way to go. I do wonder what would have happened had I stayed with one treatment all the way through (many people do with success), but I realize it was not meant to be my road to recovery. As I have said, the combination of what works is different for everyone.

I recently met a woman who has recovered from bulimia. She noted the tremendous difficulty she had in getting help, (trying one treatment option, then another) to no avail. It wasn't until she met a therapist who could work with her that she began her recovery. For example, she was an athlete and had specific needs around that issue (food and weight). Each of us has certain personal issues. It is important to understand the role they play in our disease and how we can best deal with them in recovery.

There was something comforting about being able to talk to others with similar obsessions around food, weight and all the thoughts and behaviour that go along with them. I learned that in recovery, it is extremely important to realize that you are not alone in your illness, that others have suffered and that others have made progress.

As the title of this chapter states, "Think outside the box." While traditional therapy is great, there are also a variety of other options at your disposal. For some, because of your location (a small town or village) some of the options will be easier to access than others.

(F) Non-Traditional Techniques

Following are some non-traditional treatments I tried. Each one had its benefits and collectively they helped. These techniques reduced that numbing feeling and encouraged me to be in touch with my body and my mind. The obsession with weight and food whether you suffer from anorexia, bulimia, or overeating seems to lessen when you are momentarily removed from the thought process, allowing yourself to focus on something else.

One of the "Outside the Box" techniques I experienced on my road to recovery was NLP (Neuro-Linguistic Programming). I tried this therapy over ten years ago in hopes that it would be the key to solving my illness. Again, it became another part of the recovery journey.

I am not sure how to explain this technique other than the combination of words you repeat are meant to change negative thoughts into positive ones.

I will never forget my first meeting with Dr. Shrives in Toronto. I was nervous. I knew nothing about this process other than it had helped a lot of people with a variety of mental illnesses. At this point, what did I have to lose? I will also never forget his first line to me: "I am going to ask you to repeat a series of words and sounds, and whatever you do, don't think about a blue tree." He began with the process and I was totally distracted, and he stopped. He then asked me what I was thinking about, my response: "The blue tree!" He went on to say that he had asked me not to do something and all I could think about was that negative instruction. The purpose of the therapy was to reverse this thought process.

I went to a number of sessions with Dr. Shrives and also attended some weekend ones as well. There were people there with a variety of issues from eating disorders to panic attacks. We were given exercises such as staring at someone for 5 minutes straight in the eye. Sound simple? Try it. It is quite amazing how difficult this can be. Apparently, the more comfortable you are with yourself the easier it is to do.

Other exercises included someone being put in the middle

of a circle and insulted by those around them. There were several purposes to this exercise. The person in the middle dealt with criticism in a safe environment, where he/she was aware of the fact that it was fabricated. For those around the circle, could they voice these words? Could they in fact say them, voice an opinion face to face? It was an interesting exercise; perhaps it is the element of having to face your demons. All I know is that the exercise awakened something in me. I couldn't voice the criticism. I did not want to hurt anyone's feelings.

Another interesting exercise: a sheet of paper was handed around to everyone with a variety of words and phrases on it. Different type faces of different sizes were randomly placed upon the page. We were all to describe how we viewed the page. Some saw a message. Others saw a picture. Yet others saw it as a plan or a creative piece. I saw it as a mess, disorganization that needed to be put in proper order. This simple exercise, having nothing to do with weight or food, became an indicator of my excessive need to put things in order, to have control, for things to fit into my vision.

Attending NLP sessions with Dr. Shrives became another step toward my recovery, exposing me to other methods of learning and becoming aware of myself. Dr. Shrives' influence did not stop there. He was a believer in the combination of traditional and non-traditional treatments in order to make people well in mind, body and spirit.

Soon I was attending Traggar sessions as well, a form of touch therapy. After my appointment with Dr. Shrives, he suggested Traggar as a complement to his therapy. "What the hell is that?" I said to myself. He gave a brief description of the process as touch therapy. Even the word "touch" gave me shivers, but I was desperate and was trying anything that might alleviate the pain I was feeling both inside and out. Dr. Shrives assured me that I would and could set the boundaries. The idea behind this therapy is that through touch and movement, one can open up and release pain and ease emotional struggles. The woman I was about to meet was a retired nurse now practicing Traggar. I had to keep my mind open to this and I did, but it wasn't easy.

As I got in the taxi heading from Dr. Shrives' office, I was scared and apprehensive. The taxi driver was less than pleasant, and it looked as though not taking me to my destination might be in the cards. We seemed to drive forever. All I had was a business card with an address. Keep in mind, I am not from Toronto and have no idea of the geography, so for a moment I thought I was being taken on a wild goose chase. Finally, I arrived at my destination.

But where was I? An apartment building at a dead end. When I rang the buzzer, a little Greek woman responded and welcomed me in. I took the elevator up and her apartment was the last one at the end. I will never forget the "happy face" graphic on the door. A wonderful welcome for a very frightened young lady. When she opened the door, I felt right at home. Short, round, full of life, with energy bursting at the seams, she hugged me. (Her way of placing me at ease...and it worked).

Without asking anything, she said that while normally people take off their clothes and leave on their undergarments, it was perfectly fine to leave on my entire outfit. I was greatly relieved. She spent the first few minutes discussing the process, the power of touch. She said that she often visited hospitals to help brain injured patients with their recovery. Working on their hands and fingers seemed to give a measure of comfort, with a corresponding release of energy. I remember attending a session with my husband who was willing to be a sort of guinea pig in order to display the power of touch therapy. The woman worked on one of his calves and did not work on the other. She asked him to lift the calf that she had not worked on and he couldn't lift it up. The other, the one she worked on, could be lifted, light as a feather. It was truly amazing.

It took me longer to have that comfort zone. I think because of my abuse, I was a little more sensitive to being touched. Each time I went for an appointment with Dr. Shrives, I had a Traggar appointment as well. Over time I became far more comfortable. I would literally fall asleep! It is not massage; just a very soft touch of the hands on your body. The technicians seem to sense trouble areas and work on them. For me it was a true transformation from tenseness to relaxation.

The treatment has left me very aware of the power of touch and how important it is to touch and be touched. I used to layer myself in clothing, hide from myself and everyone else. I created a wall between any human being I came in contact with, slowly removing myself from the world both physically and emotionally. If people could not touch me and if I didn't touch them, the isolation continued and it was safe. Traggar began opening me up again. Melting the ice would be a good analogy. It made me get in touch with myself, but also helped to build back that element of physical contact with people as well. I now try to hug someone whenever possible; there is something about physical connection that I have come to appreciate and value. Another thing I try to do as well is have a massage at least once a month. There is also something about having my muscles manipulated that is important.

Who knew Traggar would have the results it had when Dr. Shrives first explained it to me...another step on the road to the rainbow. Another option to consider on your road.

Another unusual exercise I did during my Traggar sessions was to use a mini trampoline. I know you are thinking, "Trampoline, why?" I know, I thought the same thing. I remember getting on the thing while Greek music began. My therapist grabbed my hands and wanted me to move with the music. My whole body was so stiff. I had become like a stone carving, numb and lifeless. Initially I would just move up and down, straight as an arrow. The instructor said that the movement would help me to be in touch with my body. After a few of these sessions, I was able to move again, to feel my joints, to feel my muscles and my body. It was new but I felt safe. It was not a cure in itself but for a moment it helped, a moment I had not had before. And I was grateful.

So you see, for me it was a combination of a variety of things, some traditional and some not in terms of the treatment route. I wanted to look at a few of these so that you might be more open to options "outside the box." There is merit in them all.

Just remember...in order for any of it to work you have to try!

CHAPTER THREE IN REVIEW

Upon reviewing this chapter perhaps the first and foremost change since I wrote the book in 2003 in reviewing this chapter has been the change from prescribed medication to organic products. When I wrote the book I was taking a 60mg dose of Prozac and had been for several years. At one point in my life I tried to go off it cold turkey (not a good idea), the side affects of doing that were horrible and any physician would tell you that it is a "no no".

What I began doing was looking into more holistic options. I began an organic regime which now includes an organic multi-vitamin (Every Woman) and organic supplements to address anxiety and stress (Holy Basil and Rhodiola Force 300) all from the line New Chapter. This is a well known company and for further information would suggest you review their web site www.newchapter.com.

It is important to note that because my diet had become extremely balanced, a lot of what I needed in terms of my chemistry was now becoming a part of my intake naturally through food. Today my nutrition and chemical balance is simply enhanced with these natural products.

I did not go cold turkey with Prozac but rather weaned myself off at a very slow pace. With any medication, as we know (prescribed or natural), you should first consult your physician.

I believe it is important to note that while I personally have now switched to organic products, Prozac served its purpose at the time and for its aid I will be forever grateful. Medications absolutely have their place, I just believe that we need to be advocates for our own health and be aware of our own body's changes and progress. We are all individuals with different needs, body chemistry and health issues. Be an advocate for yourself, take the initiative, be proactive and look after your health, you are the maestro of the orchestra!

In addition to the discussion about medication, other areas of discussion included exploration of relationships be they family, friends or an intimate relationship, breathing, documentation, hospitals, traditional and alternative therapies. The material discussed then is equally relevant today.

As we all know relationships, on whatever level, take a lot of work. The bottom line is: Are you generally happy? I say "generally" because everyday is not going to be rosy, especially when you are living under the same roof with an individual. Most importantly are you respected, cared for and loved? Can you maintain your own personal balance with this or other relationships?

As a former "people pleaser" the key for me has been to learn the valuable word "no". This response is especially useful if I feel my basic necessities for balance are being sacrificed, which are simply: sleep, moderate exercise, writing, and at least half an hour of quiet time. I have learned that it is virtually impossible to give to others unless your own basic balanced needs have been met.

Something that continues to be a very crucial ingredient in my wellness is the importance of understanding boundaries, and that very often has to do with relationships. Each of us are all very different and those boundaries will be entirely different. For me, there is an element of energy that is and isn't allowed in my life, and when I sense the negative energy is around I do what is necessary to ensure it doesn't come in. I have found that some people don't understand this concept. It is for me to understand, not them. I know what is right for me to maintain wellness and that is non-negotiable.

When I reviewed the additional material, breathing, documentation and hospital stays, along with traditional and non-traditional therapies, I am encouraged that with continued exposure and education on the disease more options are becoming available. Thankfully family physicians are becoming much more aware of signs and symptoms, and alternative/holistic options are becoming part of the collective team approach. And a team approach is crucial to wellness. By team I do not necessarily mean people but options.

A recipe for recovery varies, but it can include: work with a personal therapist, an in-house programme, a prescribed medication, a holistic option, art therapy, Traggar, yoga, body talk or NLP. Find what clicks with you; a series of those clicks will be the right recipe for you. Just remember, keep an open mind to all the possibilities, for they are truly endless.

CHAPTER FOUR

Education and Information

In addition to treatment, education is vital in battling an eating disorder. It is important in terms of the prevention and identification of the disease, the understanding and importance of treatment, as well as providing specific recovery information.

I found gathering information particularly important when it came to the physical changes to my body. Once I admitted the problem and started to read about the signs and symptoms of an eating disorder, I saw myself in the definition. For ten years I had been underweight and that was taking its toll. My entire body was deteriorating. Even though I knew the weight had to come on, I found the struggle with the weight gain overwhelming. The following journal entry in August of 1993 describes how I was feeling:

"This is what I mean, I feel frustrated, at wit's end, body grows, situation out of control and so am I. When I feel out of control, I feel somebody has put 50lbs on me and I start measuring my body.

My legs and face are getting so big but I have to keep telling myself it's muscle. I'm going to try on some pants. I really need to damn it, can't even get six of them on. I hate myself, I hit my legs hard.

I know things are moving in the right direction, being well, but I guess the biggest problem that I seem to be having are the physical changes."

I had difficulty because my body was used to being malnourished and emaciated. I was wearing children's clothing that I continued to keep. I leaned on the foundation of support by talking about how I was feeling with my therapist and writing about what was going on. It helped to release the emotional blocks and I needed verification that I was not exploding.

In 1994 I had asked Bill to take photos of me. I had gone from 78 to 104lbs but I felt huge. I couldn't see that I wasn't exploding then, but holding on to the pictures allowed me to see the truth a few years later. Had he not done that, I would have been missing vivid evidence.

 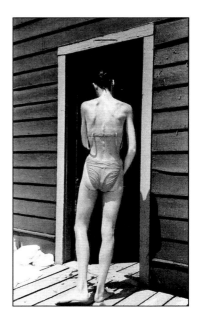

1994 reality check photograph during my road to the rainbow.
Felt 200lbs...reality, 104lbs.

I needed tangible evidence. Show me. Prove to me that I was going to be alright. Why should I need to gain the weight? I needed proof. Education and gathering information became very important in recovery. I had not menstruated for over 15 years. I needed to reacquaint myself with development. I felt in some ways like a little girl: I didn't have a period, didn't need a bra. I was concave in the chest area. When development began to return, along with my period, having accurate medical information was key. I was no longer reading about food, fat grams, calories, but rather about the body, what is necessary for healthy growth, development, and quality of life.

One author who I am particularly fond of is Dr. Christiane Northrup. Her book: *Women's Bodies, Women's Wisdom* has been like a bible for me. It is a wonderful book about women and our bodies, and I strongly recommend it.

It was important for me to gain information on the body and the need for food as fuel and what happens when there is a healthy balance. I turned to nutritionists to understand better the need for food, as well as medical information regarding everything from hunger and identifying it, to understanding some of the particular changes that were happening to my body.

What I first needed to realize was that my past behaviour had thrown my body out of whack. Finding and understanding the balance necessary was key. I had lost touch with what hunger was. I would lean on professionals and other information providers to help me find the answers.

Besides hunger, I also needed to learn and understand body set weights and appreciate the truth I had disregarded in the past. I needed to appreciate the importance of the weight gain in order for my body to be balanced and healthy. Through the aid of professionals and reading material, I realized that hunger and the feeling of being full are actually functions of the brain.

I began to understand that self starvation was burdening my body, and mechanically (as I have mentioned the car analogy before) doing tremendous damage. I learned that the restriction of food, whether avoidance or binging, was the cause of tooth decay, loss of my period, change in skin type and body temperature, as well as the cause of emotional mood swings.

Along with medical information, the reading material about others struggling with an eating disorder was also helpful. It was important to not feel alone. Also, through these materials, I learned some helpful hints regarding steps to take during recovery. Through education and speaking with those recovering, I learned how important it was to have a positive internal conversation. I keep these conversations going continually. They give me strength and keep me focused on what is real and what is important.

How do you do that? Daily quotes are a good start. Affirmations are helpful as well. Find a book that you are comfortable with. Say the affirmations and repeat them over and over again. Remember: "Fake it till you feel it."

Other tips I have read or learned along the way:

Get rid of the scale. You may do this a few times before it sticks, but it is crucial for recovery to have that temptation gone. Photos on the following page are of me at the dump in my hometown tossing in two weigh scales. That was probably the 5th time I pitched them (and it's not cheap to continually replace them). I recall once asking Bill to hide it. He did as I asked and I freaked. I turned the house upside down looking for them and proceeded to call him at his work place. The obsession is insane but keep trying. Today, they are gone. When I am around them in other people's houses or in workout areas, the temptation is no longer there. Now, I go with how I feel.

*Tossing the scales
at the local
dump...again!*

I also make sure that if I go to a doctor's appointment, and if being weighed is a part of the check up, I ask them to weigh me standing backwards. I don't need to know the number.

While getting rid of the scale is important, so is getting rid of undersized clothing. These are the articles you have held on to and could wear in the depths of your illness. The reality for me was that at 5'8" and 26 years old, wearing children's Gap clothes was just not normal, realistic or healthy. For the longest time I would hold onto particular items. I'd hide them in a drawer, use them for reference. If I could still get them on, I was okay. Slowly but surely I got rid of them, either to friends or in the garbage. It was important to give away the clothes so that they would be out of reach. Seeing them (even a child wearing your clothing) can be a temptation and a reminder. If you are just beginning recovery, it can be particularly difficult. The best suggestion is to take them to a second hand store or a thrift shop.

The idea here, as with the scale, is to get rid of triggers. In my case they were primarily the scale and small sized clothing. Getting rid of these things minimizes the clutter in your home and in your mind during recovery. Instead, you can focus on getting better. You can use the breathing techniques to help you deal with the anxiety around the changes. You can involve yourself in the community, or with a certain project, switching your control from one of an unhealthy weight obsession to elements that involve life.

I feel that both of these suggestions should be heeded by all females, eating disorder or not. There is something about the scale, and clothing you have grown out of, that serve as an agitator to a woman's mental balance. How often have you heard women say they have lost 5 pounds and appear elated, but if they have gained 5 appear depressed and irritable? Or how about discussing clothing they are wearing, whether it is snug or loose and the attitudes they possess when discussing these scenarios. Can you imagine the difference if we all collectively did not depend on the scale or a certain dress size to dictate our mood? Definitely something to think about, don't you agree?

With food, certain processes took place. I knew I had to start eating and when I did eat I had to keep it down. It started with Ensure and moved up to solid foods. Initially, it began with foods that I did not panic about. I also sometimes asked for help around food, just to have someone sit with me while I worked through all the feelings. It is important that this person is safe for you and non-judgmental. You need to be supported during this time by someone who may not understand every detail of your situation but is willing to support the process.

I had to learn to be aware of hunger. Because I had deprived myself for so long, I had lost touch with this simple human condition. This is where my journal has been particularly useful. In addition to educating myself on information regarding hunger, I wrote down the feelings about food, what hunger seemed to feel like, and how to learn when I was full, so a purge would not be the result. I wrote about physical, mental and/or emotional factors and doing so helped me immensely.

I also had to remove myself from food situations that may have been a trigger, such as buffets. Another difficult time was celebrations. Until I was ready, they were avoided. This is not always easy for others to understand but this is where information and communication are key. Maybe you need to take a rain check, then the next time tell people what you are feeling: You'd like to go but need to take your own things, or will be eating certain things, letting them know in advance so they are aware. It helps everyone understand. This step is awkward, especially with people who are uncomfortable with your disease or your process of recovery. Some people accepted this step of my recovery, while others did not. You have to surround yourself with the people who will.

Another indicator I had to recognize in my journals was the influence of alcohol on my feelings and behaviour, particularly during a bulimic stage. When my body weight was low, alcohol seemed to help numb everything even more, but it did not make it better. I was malnourished and alcohol did not help. It can also be the trigger for a binge and purge. While recovering, it can add to the problem and delay recovery.

It will get easier. Just keep trying. As I have said many

times throughout this book, the good moments continue to add up. You will notice changes in your journals, how you feel about yourself, how you feel about your body and how you feel about life.

In 1993 I wrote, *"I made it thru last night...ya hoo!"*

In 1997, *"Holding on really well. I can't ever remember three days of normalcy like I've been having. What has been different? Talking to myself positively, I'm worth the effort, to try in hopes of living a normal life with no more missed opportunities. It is much better when I don't weigh myself or wear clothing that's constricting or too small. Reading Louise Hay's The Power is Within You, and Don't Sweat the Small Stuff."*

Oct 4, 2000, *"Go girl! You did it Mer and see how much better you feel too. Yep I feel great. So up and at 'em. Things are moving in a great direction, and I am so very excited."*

It is hard to imagine the above journal entry is by the same person who wrote the obituary you read at the beginning of this book. I have to pinch myself sometimes as well.

I have said before about an eating disorder: "Meet it, greet it, defeat it."

Education and information will help through each stage of recovery. It serves as a wonderful addition to therapy and serves as the tangible evidence needed for successful recovery.

I read several books on a variety of topics related to my disorders, and issues related to it. Some of the books that helped in particular include; *A Time To Be Free* (author anonymous), *Awareness Through Movement* by Moshe Feldenfrais, *You Can Become the Person You Want to Be* by Robert Schuller, *Mind Over Mood* by Dennis Greenberger and Christine A. Padesky, *The Courage to Heal Workbook* by Laura Davis, *Showing Up for Life* by Heidi Waldrop, and *Bulimia* by Lindsey Hall and Leigh Cohn.

CHAPTER FOUR IN REVIEW

In this chapter I discussed the importance of educating yourself about the body and how it works in order to understand why you need to eat properly.

Now education and information has shifted for me from eating disorder information to literature that can help with supporting and encouraging a stronger me from the inside out.

Over the last five years I have really done a lot of work on developing the core and spirit of my being and it has and continues to be a wonderful journey into self exploration.

I find reading the literature of authors like Eckhart Tolle, Wayne Dyer and Marianne Williamson extremely comforting and centering. They, through their words, have made me appreciate the peace of just being and the real appreciation of being present in the moment. Often when I find myself getting caught up in the business of a day I will re-group by reading one of these authors and am soon present in the world of what matters most, right now.

So often we as human beings worry about what we didn't do yesterday or worry about what needs to be done tomorrow; in the meantime we miss all the opportunities that are present in what is the now. I am learning that to be present is the key to a fulfilled life. If you are trying to be the best you can be in the moment mentally, physically, emotionally and spiritually, the rest of it all seems to take care of itself.

Much of the reading has to do with the ego and its deception of what is really important. It gets us off track and brings with it hatred, jealousy, anger, resentment and the list goes on. When we just get in touch with the core and peaceful spirit of a higher power (and that can mean many things ie. God, Buddha, etc.) life seems to just make sense. I have found that when I stay centered and present life works out. When I get distracted and let little things get in the way the further I get from what matters, the further I get from calm and peace. Sometimes all it takes are a few words from the aforementioned authors or perhaps a quiet moment with some positive important self talk to snap back. Unless you explore this journey it will seem out of reach. The grasp is closer than you think.

Another book I encourage you to read which I have previously mentioned is *The Secret* by Rhonda Byrne. The premise is that the secret to life is really based on one law, "The Law of Attraction". The idea is that what you radiate out you will receive. I have mentioned this concept in the 2003 edition of this book (prior to The Secret's publication) and in this edition as well. If you practice even a simple test of smiling at someone watch what happens…they smile back. Shoot an angry glare, watch the result. It really is true, where you focus your energy you will see the results.

I personally believe that this law of attraction, in combination with a centered, grounded core is key to personal peace allowing one to live a full, wonderful life. A part of me wishes these works were available in my deepest hours but positively I believe the timing has been meant to be during this phase of my life; partly for me but more importantly to pass on their importance to you.

CHAPTER FIVE

Journaling

The most important aid in my recovery has been journaling. Not only has it served as the research backbone of this book, but it has also allowed me to chronicle both my illness and my life. It has been a keeper of my disease development and steps towards recovery, but also of history, births, deaths, celebrations, special letters, photographs and moments to remember.

For over twenty years I have kept these journals. Here are a few lessons about journal writing I have learned along the way:

1. Journals are private

Many people have said to me, "Don't write anything in a journal that you don't want others to see." I do not agree. Journals are private and not meant to be shared without your permission. When you are ill as I was, those who love you may want to read them to help them understand. Not a good idea. I would write the good, the bad and the ugly about how I was feeling. On a given day, I may have a real issue with someone close to me. The journal is where I could and would vent without hurting others. My journal was crucial for my therapy sessions as well. I had a record of a certain situation at a particular time and noted my feelings at that particular time. It is important to express without judgement. This is particularly important because at the height of my illness, my own judgement was impaired, but still needed to be expressed. It is important to get the feelings out.

When someone else reads your journal, a trust and a bond is broken no matter the intent. Should he/she be forgiven because of desperation to help and understand you? Probably, but depending on the information, it can often not be forgotten by either party.

I stress the importance of boundaries with your journals. When you live alone it is much easier to have complete privacy with your journals, but if you are a child still at home with parents and siblings, or living with a spouse or a roommate, establishing privacy is very important. It may be important to have a locked journal, a special place, or a secure location. Whatever the boundaries, they are crucial in order for you to use the journal as an honesty pit. If you can't be honest in your journals, I am afraid their use as a recovery tool will be limited.

I see through my own journals that recovery seemed to begin when I began not only being honest with myself, but also seeing the truth in print. What I was feeling became particularly real when I could see it on the page. I really was able to see this as I reviewed my journals for this book. Being able to revisit the desperation, the self loathing, the hatred and obsessions and how they lessened with proper nutrition and weight gain has made my recovery all the more real. I have not only seen the results, I have tracked them. I have recognized that recovery has been a slow process, but it is indeed possible.

Journals need to be private in order for you to explore not only yourself and your feelings but all that is around you. Establishing that privacy is crucial.

2. Journals allow you to be creative: the importance of artwork

I used journals to write and to doodle, collect things, store photographs and memorabilia. It is interesting when you go back and review what you wrote, drew and saved. It gives you a real sense of where you were and where you are.

I think it is important to allow yourself to be creative in your journal because there is something liberating and empowering about doing this. Artistic expression can be very therapeutic. Often I felt trapped in terms of verbal expression. Art became a wonderful substitute instead of stifling those feelings and ignoring them. I remember during one of my hospital visits feeling as though I was hollow, with nothing to live for. Nothing mattered. I was numb. I also couldn't say what I felt because I didn't know. I was so out of touch with myself at that time. How could I possibly explain it to someone else? The journal allowed me to express my feelings and the artwork illustrated the pain.

The Wanderer

I kept my artwork and one piece in particular reminds me of my pain. I had drawn a woman walking into the water with no face, no feet and no hands. I remember feeling the inability to see, to recognize myself, feeling unable to touch, feel, or move, as if I was paralyzed in my body both physically and mentally. Journals can be a keeper of emotional and artistic expression. When I was afraid and blocked, journals helped me to release that energy.

3. Journals are an adaptable therapy

I suppose the most wonderful thing about journals is their versatility. They can go anywhere. If you have to go away and if you are in therapy, it allows you to consistently keep track of those feelings and thoughts. It is with you no matter what the event or emotion. It is non-judgmental and confidential. Also, journals serve as an aid to your recovery. I often used mine in therapy to discuss with my therapist the thoughts and feelings of a particular time. Journals assist you in letting others help you (if you choose to do so) and they assist you to help yourself.

Be honest in these journals. It won't always make a lot of sense. (I look back on a lot of mine and many are a total mess. I couldn't tell you what I had written but I sure knew I was upset.) There will come a time when sense will be made of this confusion.

Try using your journal as a tracker. Often if I had a bad day, I would try to go back and see what it was that made things turn sour. Was it a comment? What was I feeling about myself at that moment, mentally and physically? Had anything happened the previous day or evening that could have influenced my behaviour? The important thing to remember is that you have a right to your thoughts and feelings. They are neither right nor wrong. At that particular time, they are yours and what you are feeling. Recovery is recognizing the reality of those feelings. Often, when I was very ill, my feelings seemed to be hyper sensitive, reacting to anything. I felt paranoid, resentful and angry at everything and everybody. It would not matter what a person said, I would twist it to mean something about me, related to my life. "They didn't like me, hated me. I wasn't good at anything. Why were they doing this to me?"

I had to go through that time. I had to write about what I was feeling, and I am glad I did. I can now see the correlation between low weight, erratic eating behaviour (avoidance of food or binging and purging) and those thoughts and feelings. As the weight gain occurred and erratic behaviour lessened, so did those feelings. I see a definite correlation. I know if I had not kept a journal, the reality of the correlation would have been far more difficult to comprehend. Throughout my illness, family, friends and the medical fraternity tried to stress to me the correlation between a normal body weight and realistic perceptions, but I didn't believe or trust anyone.

My journals helped me to believe.

The truth cannot lie.

During therapy, the journal notes what is important and thereby influences your recovery. Sleep became very important in my recovery. When I was very ill, on the rare occasion that I got a good night's sleep, it was remarkable how much better equipped I was to deal with things the following day.

It kept occurring in my journals. Just as calm in my home resulted in a better day, so too did waking up well rested. It often dictated how the day was going to unfold. If my sleep was disturbed, the first thing I did was weigh myself, sometimes at 4 am. Then I'd just stay up, do some exercising, and weigh myself again. If an eating function was planned for later in the day, a binge and purge cycle would result.

What help resulted in a better night's sleep?

A pattern for the day was part of the answer. It was important for me to get up and get moving. This could be as simple as going for a walk. A purpose in the morning was essential.

About exercise: For me it has been a key to recovery. What I have had to do is be sensible about the amount of exercise. At one point it would have been common to do hours of step and then walk 10 miles. But the years of abuse to my body have taken their toll. Knees and other joints are not what they used to be, and I have had to adjust my exercise regime to one of moderation. My daily routine enhances my life but does not control my life. I exercise now because I like it. I try to walk at least half an hour each day (with weights three times a week).

Through my journals, I have seen that if I have not exercised or moved for a few days, my mood and my sleep patterns seem to be disrupted. I also believe exercise has helped to deal with the necessary weight gain and to combat osteoporosis, often the result of a long-term eating disorder.

Nothing helps me more at the end of the day than a hot bath. This may seem an obvious thing but when I was very ill and very thin, I was always cold and more comfortable wearing layers of clothes. I would be in them for days. I'd sleep in them and do the same thing the next day and the next. Having a bath had more meaning than basic cleanliness. It forced me to be in touch with myself. It forced me to avoid the numbness temporarily, to feel the heat of the water, and to feel my body.

Also important was being dressed in clean clothes and putting myself together to go out. Because of my illness, I was off work on disability for many years and had no incentive to leave my house. Therefore, anything that provided incentive, even if it was a doctor's appointment, was important.

This aspect of getting "up and at 'em" along with putting one's best foot forward is something I try to do everyday and when I do not, I certainly notice the difference. Just do the test yourself. Check out your mood and mind set during a day of no bathing, staying in your sweats, avoiding the world and staying in, versus getting up, bathing, dressing (in something you are comfortable in) and going out. See the difference? Track it in a journal. I think you will be surprised by the results.

When I was busy for the day, my life seemed full for the moment. When I stayed home and didn't go anywhere, it was exhausting. Doing something for someone else, such as volunteering, took the focus off me, and that helped. There are so many worthwhile causes out there. Pick an interest. Lend a hand. Find a purpose.

I would come back at the end of the day feeling in touch with the environment around me. Connecting to the world and normalcy seemed to help. Through my journals, I saw that being busy was key. Boredom signalled trouble.

Journal entries also indicated that eating lighter meals in the evening was better. I find combining a protein with a vegetable seems to work best. Also, eat early and slowly.

Make sure you are sleeping in a fresh bed. There is something about crashing on a fresh pillow case that can't be beat.

It seems obvious that being sleep deprived leads to physical and mental unrest, but I mention it because I so often noted it in my journals. Maybe someone reading this has never acknowledged the importance of sleep. The recognition may make a difference. I hope it does.

4. The actual journal...be sure it's user friendly

I cannot stress enough the importance of how you feel about the journal. If you are not comfortable with it, it will seem like a stranger. Just as some people prefer hardcover books to paperbacks, so too, are there preferences regarding journals.

I prefer journals with rings. I like being able to fold them over. To me it's more comfortable if I am on a train or plane to deal with one side instead of an open book. When given non-ringed journals for gifts, I tend to write on the right side and attach mementoes to the left.

I also like journals with inspirational or thought provoking quotes. I also appreciate journals with a place to store photographs or letters. Most importantly, a journal should be comfortable. Along with your journal, pick a pen that flows with you and not against you. Believe me when I say that your journal will not only be a sounding board but will become a confidant and a friend on your road to the rainbow.

Journals let you see where the darkness lies. Used in conjunction with a variety of treatment methods, journals become another important tool in your recovery.

Journaling continues to serve not only as a wonderful sounding board for me but a great record keeper of my life and of the lives of those special people who make my world complete.

I continue to use my journal as a sounding board especially in times of stress or questioning. There is something therapeutic about writing out what I am thinking that helps me move to the next step. During times of question I often write then read out loud the written words. Something about the process just helps to see the situation clearer or at the very least more realistically. Weighing the options on the page can be very helpful. Sometimes when I read the written words I feel, "Yep, I'm on the right track." Other times…"What are you talking about?" Always a process…always worthwhile.

What is kind of interesting since I wrote the book is that all the journals I had documenting intake/out-take of food and exercise, and the dark feelings of despair, were all burned on my 40th birthday. Yep, all of them!

On my 40th, I had a wonderful day. I went for a long walk; it was beautiful out. Laid out by the pool by my apartment then headed to my brother's where a large fire bin was ready for me. My brother and two nephews helped to tear and burn the pain of the past. It was kind of funny actually as my youngest nephew while catching a glimpse of an entry said, "Aunt Mer, why do you have the word 'Fuck' all over these pages?" Out of the mouth's of babes. There was something in his question that just made the reality of the past pain so real but more importantly, so over. With each journal, and there were many, there was a sense of closure. I had already used them to help write the book. There was no need to further be reminded of the dark; life was now about the light.

As mentioned, my journal writing still serves as a wonderful aid, a personal therapist I can take anywhere. But I also keep track of life's wonderful events in order to share reminders of those times with family and friends at Christmas and special birthdays. The days are now filled with life and all its wonders.

These pages of light are just waiting for you.

CHAPTER SIX

Importance of Your Environment

One thing that became evident while reviewing my journals was the importance of my environment, my physical environment.

Often in my journals, I would write about how much better I felt when my home was in order and clean. There seemed to be a definite parallel between chaos and my mood. There was something about cleaning that seemed to clear the cobwebs in my home and in my head. This is something I am very aware of today as well. When my home is in order, I feel in order. There is a calmness and a peace and a sense of accomplishment, which for me, is essential. It became a positive healthy sense of control.

When I talk about this type of cleaning, it isn't just a lick and a promise, but really getting at it. I mean cleaning out drawers, baseboards, cupboards, the dishes inside, glass, floors and stains off carpets. I came by this cleaning habit honestly, but my journals let me see the importance of it. It provided a sense of purpose and accomplishment. In the scope of things, this is not earth shattering, but it has served as an important ingredient in my recovery. There is something about order, cleanliness and the fresh smell that brings you back to reality. Instead of covering things up, or having dust layering everything around you, you feel clean when items around you are clean. It does something.

I also learned the importance of colour in my environment and its affect on my mood. Initially in my home, I had dark colours (very dark...burgundies, browns). I thought they were warm but I realized they helped me to hibernate. On a bad day, it was easy to pull the blinds down and put the covers over my head. I would not know or care if it was a beautiful day. I remember creating a colourful bedroom with primary colours. I rarely went in there. It was almost as if I wanted it but fought it at the same time. I think back on it and feel as though I was becoming completely comfortable living with this disease. I did not want to feel the light or feel the sunshine.

But what happened when I did?

The results have been amazing.

Light and sunshine have always brought me back to reality. It stops the numbing, like a heating pad being applied to your skin. And there is definitely something about light. In the winter, or during a stretch of rainy days, I make sure I head to the tanning booth. This tip may not be of benefit to you (and dermatologists would challenge me, I am sure), but it has worked for me. In the summer, I try to be outside as much as possible. I love everything about the summer and how it makes me feel. When I was very thin and very ill, the sun seemed to warm not only my skin but my soul. I continue to need that light, that energy and that warmth.

I now incorporate light in my home (not dark colours, but light ones...whites and creams). I also have lots of light. Windows are uncovered, letting in as much natural light as possible.

I have also filled my home with things that remind me of positive happenings. I'm surrounded by photographs of happy times and happy people: people I feel good about, and who feel good about me. In each room there are positive poems or messages, reminders of the specialness of life. I dedicate one room to this "positive energy". Recently a new acquaintance who had never been in my home said, "What the heck is this...a self help room?" My response? "It works for me." And there is the difference. Even 5 years ago I would have been devastated by such a comment. Now, because I am so comfortable in my own skin, I just take it for what it is...an observation. At times like that I realize how far I've come.

One poem that hangs framed in this room is very special to me. Written by Virginia Satir in her book *Self Esteem,* the poem is entitled *I Am Me!* It reminds me that I am an individual, unique in the world, and that is what makes me and each of us special. It reminds me of my individuality as well as my strength and my personal power. I have often read it during presentations. I find it inspirational and I hope it may serve as support for you as well.

We each have the power and the strength to get better. Surround yourself with positive messages like this and the negative messages fade into the background. Just give it a try!

I also buy flowers at least once a week. Even if I buy just one, there is something special about its freshness and smell, its simple beauty. If I get more than one, I put them throughout my apartment. One trick I have learned to help them last longer is to put a few drops of bleach in the water.

The work environment is also very important. Even if you are in a cubicle you can surround yourself with colour, photographs, illustrations and flowers. Besides the actual work environment, it is essential to like what you do and who you work with. I am not saying you need to be elated every moment, but contented would be a good start. It can have a huge effect on your well-being and your recovery. If you are unhappy at work, ask for a new task or consider a career change. It might be the answer you are looking for.

Another very important environmental influence on me has been water. (Not the drinking variety, but bodies of water: rivers, lakes and streams...any body of water with movement).

Often I would write in my journal how much better I felt after I had walked by the water, sat on a beach, or just gazed at the river from a dock. There is something so unending about a body of water and the calming sound of the waves. There is an element of peace to hear the birds and to watch the clouds move sometimes slowly, sometimes swiftly through the sky. The sense of water, when I was ill, was bigger than I was; bigger than the disease. For a moment the pain went away. It was good to feel that.

I often took that time to write in my journal, especially if it had been a tough day. I could be quite anxious with a feeling of panic coming over me, but taking the pen and finding a comfortable spot by the water allowed me to calm down and let out, in a healthy environment, what I was thinking and feeling. Water always seemed to let those feelings and thoughts flow.

Music has also been a part of my life and has served as an important function in my recovery. Through journals I came to realize that when I listened to soft music first thing in the morning, as opposed to the news, a positive influence resulted. The environment was calm and served as a type of leveller to start the day. Some of the artists I continue to listen to include: James Taylor, Diana Krall, Natalie Cole, Billie Holiday and Dan Hill. James Taylor is my favourite, particularly in the morning. For me, he is particularly calming and I usually listen to him during my walks as well.

It's been my experience that you do not need to make huge changes in your environment. Just be aware of the importance of how your environment affects your mood.

Chapter Six in Review

Upon reviewing this chapter it is interesting to note almost a growth spurt, as I can't think of another way to describe it.

I discussed in this chapter the power of a positive environment and one that is created for you that is safe, secure and calm no matter the size. Those points are equally important for me today at my home and my workplace.

Fairly recently I gave my apartment that I have been living in now for almost ten years a total facelift. I gave it a life by painting with some new colours, added new curtains as well as some wonderful little touches resulting in an entirely new feel to an old space.

Perhaps most interesting was the de-cluttering process. The entire apartment was painted so I had to move everything and it gave me the opportunity to really re-evaluate the items in my home and the "need" for them now. Clutter and stuff can be stifling and overwhelming, and what a euphoric feeling it was to rid myself of the "stuff".

When this chapter was first written I discussed the importance of quotes and the many framed ones in my apartment. Once I began the cleaning process for painting I took everything off the walls and only a select few were put back up. I can't really explain it other than it was time to move on. The framed printed quotes had had a very special purpose at one time, but it was time to move on, move forward.

I would encourage everyone to take some time to de-clutter. Perhaps on a rainy day you'll decide to tackle a kitchen drawer or a closet. Give it a shot. Really ask yourself if you need it. If not, then give it away. This serves two purposes: it de-clutters your life, and possibly at the same time it helps someone else.

CHAPTER SEVEN

Going Public

I cap off my story of recovery by stressing the over-whelming power sharing one's story can have on recovery. Sharing your stages of recovery can help someone who has not yet reached your stage of wellness. When you share your story, hope is shared and the strength is doubled.

Every time I have spoken publicly about my eating disorders and the process of recovery, the disease lost more power. My first presentation was back in 1996 to a high school in Ottawa. I was nervous. Nervous not only about the presentation, but about verbalizing the truth about my disease, where I was, where I was going and the future of my life. At times the presentations have been painful but always worthwhile. I have also done television interviews and a few newspaper and radio interviews as well. It gets the problem out there.

Speaking out challenges the demons within and shows the disease I have won and it hasn't.

Writing this book has been the ultimate in truth for me. It has been at times very sad, but in the end a triumph. I have found my purpose and found my passion: It is to share my story, share my recovery, share the reality of a healthy, happy life.

After a presentation in 1999 I received the following letter:

Dear Meredith,

I just wanted to let you know how much I enjoyed your talk at the February meeting. I found it so very moving and have since thought about it a lot.

You are one special person to have come through what you did and to share this terrible time in your life with others. I am sure this knowledge you gave us will be of help to one of us sometime in the future.

With all the notes you kept over the years, you should seriously think of putting this in a book. I am sure a book would be of great assistance to others afflicted with this illness, recovering and their loved ones.

Keep recovering and my prayers are with you for a healthy future.

Yours in Networking,
Shirley

Shirley, I have heeded your advice, and thank you.

I know when I was ill I wanted to meet someone who said it was over. Someone who knew the struggles, the pain and the anxiety, but had crossed the hump, made it over the hill. I have finally met her...

It's me!

All my life I have felt a purpose. Each of us has one. I know now that mine is to share and help. To let you believe that wellness is indeed an option...the option.

The road you travel to your rainbow will be different from mine, but the techniques and principles I have used can be adapted to suit you and your support system. Just please don't give up, and don't be discouraged. With time, drive and

determination to be well, health will be the result.
Remember rainbows, remember........

> *You cannot climb high mountains*
> *Before you've walked low ground*
> *And on the road to wisdom*
> *No short cuts can be found*
> *Have courage in adversity*
> *You will not strive in vain*
> *There never was a rainbow*
> *Without a fall of rain.*

CHAPTER SEVEN IN REVIEW

I continue to share my story of recovery with the public and truly believe that the sharing of our recovery stories is monumental in its ability to help many.

On the topic of going public, a fairly interesting chain of events happened since writing the book. I had sent my book to Woman's World magazine in the United States the year I published the book in the hopes they would cover the story. Knowing that they printed a rare few from thousands of submissions you can imagine my surprise and delight when they contacted me to say it was a go. I was excited about the exposure of my story and the opportunity to tell thousands and potentially millions about the story of hope and recovery.

The magazine went to the expense of sending a photographer to my home for pictures and a small fee to me before the interview. On the day of the interview the line of questioning was shocking to me. Their main concern was wanting to know the weigh scale numbers and my food intake. I had to ask the interviewer, "Have you read the book?" The answer was "no". I ended up telling the interviewer that if she had read the book she would be aware that it was about how to get better, not about encouraging the obsessions with a number on a scale and food intake. I said thanks but no thanks for the coverage if that would be the approach to the article.

As a self-published author with limited funds to spread my message of hope, it is needless to say how disappointed I was that it didn't work out. But through that experience a very special thing happened. The photographer who was hired through a Canadian company in Toronto was processing my pictures and talking to a producer about my story. The producer who was working on a television series called

"Second Chance," a series covering women who had overcome adversities, asked if he thought I may be interested in being interviewed for the program. The photographer called me and I said, "Absolutely!"

The production company called and wanted to interview all my family members, friends and physicians. I checked and everyone was in; anything they could do to help others was their response. The team came, spent a few days with us, and the show aired across the country. It continues to air and continues to help people.

I watched the program alone here at home. You have to remember, I was not present during any of the other interviews so when the final product aired I was moved to tears. Today, when I watch the program during presentations I still tear up at the life of pain. Not only about myself but family and friends, and yet I always end the program with a wide smile knowing that we have all overcome the pain. It is a wonderful story of hope for all and to Woman's World magazine, in a very strange way I will be forever grateful.

To share our stories of hope is essential, as it is to share with a sufferer; and please know that it can make all the difference in the world to a degree that you can't possibly imagine.

I would like to finish my review of *Road to the Rainbow* with a very special letter written to me. This letter is written by a young woman whom I was able to share and support through my story, a true example of pay it forward…

125

*The very least you can do in your life
is to figure out what you hope for.
And the most you can do is live inside that hope.
Do not admire it from a distance but
live right in it, under its roof.*
- Barbara Kingsolver

*"For fifteen years, more than half my life, I have
been anorexic. The disease had consumed me and my
life. Every moment was devoted to my sickness. I was
angry. I was scared. I was lonely. I was starving, not
just in the physical sense, but in a spiritual sense. I had
given up hope and I made up my mind to turn myself
fully over to anorexia, giving up any pretence of a
normal life. Anorexia was my life, it was my identity.
There was no point in hoping for anything else.*

*I spiralled even further out of control, isolated
myself from everything and began living solely for my
disease. My parents were terrified and insisted I come
home to try and get well. I agreed, after many tears and
temper tantrums.*

*I had, in the past, had periods when I had been at a
healthy weight. My mind, however, was never healthy.
Those voices in my head never shut off and I became
resigned to the fact that I would always be sick. I would
never be able to just live. I would always have to battle
and in the end, anorexia would probably get me.*

*My parents wanted me to speak with a woman they
had seen on a television program. Like me, she had
gone through anorexia. I wasn't too thrilled with this
idea, agreeing only to get my mom and dad off my case.
With great reservation, I went to speak with her.*

The first thing that struck me about Meredith was

that she radiated joy, something I could not understand. How could she be happy without her disease? For the life of me, I could not comprehend how she could live her life without those voices cropping up, those urges taking over. It just wasn't possible.

The thing is, the more time I spent with her, the more I realized that yes, it is possible. This gave me great hope, hope that I could pull through this and live a normal life. I began to hope for the first time since I was thirteen years old that I could face the world as my true self, not as my disease. She made me realize that I am not my illness. It was a scary thought at first, but the further I pushed myself, the more excited I became. Revelation after revelation came to me and it was as if I was meeting myself for the first time. I had stopped living at thirteen. The only emotions I had felt in years were anger and hate. Suddenly I noticed that I was smiling and people were smiling back! Each day I would discover something new, and I began taking pleasure in the small things in life.

While my body changed into that of a woman instead of a mal-nourished pre-pubescent girl, I took delight in how strong my legs were now. They didn't feel like they would give out at any moment. My heart beat in a steady rhythm. My joints didn't ache.

I was feeding my body, but most importantly, I was feeding my soul. I had hope. I had a life outside the disease and I liked it! Anorexia would not take me. I wouldn't let it back into my life ever again because I now know what it is like to live free, unafraid and unashamed. I was content and at peace with myself.

I know now why Meredith radiated joy; it comes from a wonder for life, of experiencing moments that went ignored for years and years. Nothing is taken for granted and not one day can pass by without being thankful to be free of the prison of anorexia. I know it is possible to live in the sun, free from the prison. Meredith is proof, and now, I am too."

The power of hope is overwhelming, and my wish as I conclude is that this powerful chain of hope…continues with you.

LIST OF HELPFUL RESOURCES

Literature/Books

The Secret by Rhonda Byrne
Inspiration Your Ultimate Calling by Dr. Wayne Dyer
The Power of Intention by Dr. Wayne Dyer
The Awakened Life by Dr. Wayne Dyer
Change Your Thoughts Change Your Life by Wayne Dyer
The Power is Within You by Lousie L. Hay
The Power of Now by Eckhart Tolle
A New Earth by Eckhart Tolle
Stillness Speaks by Eckhart Tolle
The Age of Miracles by Marianne Williamson
The Four Agreements by Don Miguel Ruiz
The Four Agreements Companion Book by Don Miguel Ruiz
Succulent Wild Woman by Sark
The Seat of the Soul by Gary Zukav
The Five Love Languages by Gary Chapman
The Power of Your Subconscious Mind by Dr. Joseph Murphy, revised by Ian McMahane
Mind Over Mood: Change How You Feel by Changing the Way You Think by Dennis Greenberger, Christine Padesky
Feeding the Soul: Daily Meditations for Those Recovering from Eating Disorders by Caroline Adams Miller

Resources/Web Pages

Canada

Sheena's Place:
www.sheenasplace.org
Kids Help Line:
www.kidshelpphone.ca
The Centre for Addiction and Mental Health:
www.camh.net
National Eating Disorder Information Centre (NEDIC):
www.nedic.ca

United States

National Eating Disorders Association (NEDA):
www.edap.org
Eating Disorder Referral and Information Center:
www.nationaleatingdisorders.org
Gurze Books – Specializing in Eating Disorders
Publications and Education:
www.gurze.com

United Kingdom

National Centre for Eating Disorders:
www.eating-disorders.org.uk

CONTACT THE AUTHOR

Meredith Seafield Grant may be contacted directly through her web site at:

www.roadtotherainbow.com

Likewise, you may write to her directly by e-mail at:

msg@seafield.org

Printed by BoD™in Norderstedt, Germany

9 780980 919172